T0121374

CONSCIOUSLY CONNECTING

• • • • • • • • • • • • • • • • • • •

A Simple Process to Reconnect
in a Disconnected World

Holland Haiis

BALBOA.
PRESS

A DIVISION OF HAY HOUSE

Copyright © 2014 Holland Haiis.

All rights reserved. No part of this book may be used or reproduced by any means, graphic, electronic, or mechanical, including photocopying, recording, taping or by any information storage retrieval system without the written permission of the publisher except in the case of brief quotations embodied in critical articles and reviews.

Balboa Press books may be ordered through booksellers or by contacting:

Balboa Press
A Division of Hay House
1663 Liberty Drive
Bloomington, IN 47403
www.balboapress.com
1 (877) 407-4847

Because of the dynamic nature of the Internet, any web addresses or links contained in this book may have changed since publication and may no longer be valid. The views expressed in this work are solely those of the author and do not necessarily reflect the views of the publisher, and the publisher hereby disclaims any responsibility for them.

The author of this book does not dispense medical advice or prescribe the use of any technique as a form of treatment for physical, emotional, or medical problems without the advice of a physician, either directly or indirectly. The intent of the author is only to offer information of a general nature to help you in your quest for emotional and spiritual well-being. In the event you use any of the information in this book for yourself, which is your constitutional right, the author and the publisher assume no responsibility for your actions.

Any people depicted in stock imagery provided by Thinkstock are models, and such images are being used for illustrative purposes only.
Certain stock imagery © Thinkstock.

Printed in the United States of America.

ISBN: 978-1-4525-9785-0 (sc)
ISBN: 978-1-4525-9787-4 (hc)
ISBN: 978-1-4525-9786-7 (e)

Library of Congress Control Number: 2014919316

Balboa Press rev. date: 12/08/2014

This book is dedicated to my mentor
and friend, my mother.

Contents

• • • • • • • •

OCTOBER: HARVEST THE CHANGES

NOVEMBER: THANKFUL FOR YOUR TREASURES

DECEMBER: TIME FOR CELEBRATION

THE CULMINATION, A.K.A. THE CONTINUUM

ACKNOWLEDGMENTS

· · · · · · · · · · · · · · · · · · ·

Love and thanks to my mother, who clearly understands the difference between preaching and teaching, pushing and nudging, loving and smothering. Your grace, gratitude, and humility have taught me well. Your effortless joy and wonder of the world are both beguiling and contagious.

And, love and thanks to my husband, you make marching to your own beat so cool. I am grateful to you for making your journey east, on the condition I continue my creative journey within.

There is no amount of gratitude to thank Alison Yobage and Josette Galtieri-Green for the painstaking task of editing my every word and inconsistency with kindness and care. You have both loved this baby as if it were your own!

I am grateful for the many people who have passed through my life, either in turmoil, bliss, or by way of tsunami. You have forced me to swim oceans when I thought I could only cross a river, fight wars when I was barely capable of a battle, and spend months in a storm when all I wanted was sunshine. Thank you, for now I swim, fight, survive, and rejoice due to your blessings.

INTRODUCTION

• • • • • • • • • • • • •

In the age of technology we have become disconnected at a cellular level. The time to reconnect to ourselves and each other is now!

One of my many wake-up calls came in the middle of Central Park when I was more interested in emails than enjoying the beauty of my surroundings. Heck, I could not tell you what was happening five feet in front of me. Considering that my usual radar extends nearly a mile, in all directions, this was some strange new territory that was becoming all too familiar. It is common practice for many in New York City to stop random strangers from walking into traffic, due to their momentary disconnection, and I too have been saved from what could have been a catastrophic collision with a swiftly passing taxi or bus on more than a few occasions. And while at the point of full disclosure, I have also been one of those drivers more interested in emails and texting than the road before me—literally and figuratively. It's understood that technology is here to stay, but like everything in life it is about balance, and the scales have tipped on this one.

You may not know how or why you have arrived at the precipice of disconnection. I didn't, but I knew one thing for sure: it was time to step away from the cliff. I have spent decades facilitating others to connect deeper into their businesses and teaching the psychology of marketing strategies and how to build a team and bridge the financial gaps, but suddenly the bridge to my own connections needed some repair. I proceeded to pay careful attention to how often I disconnected from being present in business or even my personal life for that matter. I observed my own disconnect happening during coffee with friends as I eagerly checked my incoming emails and texts, all halting the flow of precious time with one another.

While almost everyone in the world would agree we are more technologically connected than we have ever been, we are simultaneously the most disconnected as well. The twentieth century has given us the wonderful gift of technology, connecting us in more ways than we ever dreamed possible. In return, many have dismissed the ability to connect to anything other than technology, and so we are falling further into the abyss of disconnection. Technology has put everything at our fingertips, within seconds we have more knowledge than our grandparents did after two hours in a library. Our connection to technology has become our new addiction. It is imperative that we find our way back.

The disconnection in my life did not terminate with the issues surrounding technology. I was constantly winding up with daily to-do lists that never seem to dissipate. Being exhausted before the day begins, constantly feeling overtired, and running on caffeine leaves much to be desired. I also experienced disconnects from what was eaten and how it was eaten, but I too wanted to eat cheese and drink wine like the French! Maybe you're out of practice, but it's easy to connect back into the quality time to enjoy beautiful meals as you slow down and learn to release the distractions.

Hearing friends moan and groan while aging in their twenties, thirties, and forties has often had me questioning, "Why do we all end up feeling this way?" And while my husband continues to remind me that each year it is my tenth, eleventh, maybe fourteenth attempt at perfecting the age of thirty-six, the realization has set in—we will all eventually age and it is okay. But the real question is why we, as a collective, are unable to embrace the wisdom that comes with age? The effect of tricky advertising dissuades and shames those few gray hairs, weighing ten extra pounds, and getting "older." All too easily the spell of disappointment has been cast and chasing the elixirs that promise everlasting youth further add to the disconnect. Rather than connecting to the gift of maturity, which has been bestowed by the knowledge of lessons learned and conquered, the chasm widens as real beauty is second-guessed.

Much of the reason I enjoy foreign travel and a good adventure is the opportunity to slow down and reconnect to myself and others. Unfolding into the enjoyment of visiting small towns with a slower pace, relaxing during a two-hour lunch, and leisurely enjoying a cup of coffee sets me on the path to the holy grail of connection through my environment and experiences. I can peer into the window of a more relaxed lifestyle by imagining endless possibilities. Europeans commune with food and friends in a leisurely manner as they look forward to these exchanges while they recharge for what lies ahead. Americans put in long hours and continue to stay connected to all sorts of technology well into evenings and weekends. I saw I was not allowing myself to disengage from these tools and that it was leading me to further disconnection. It's no wonder as a collective and individually we feel out of sync and crave something else for our lives but don't know exactly how to plug in and reconnect.

We are all experiencing the slow drifting into the land of saturation and overload that makes it difficult to connect to ourselves and one another. A craving for simplicity has registered in the collective subconscious, although I'm not quite sure it's in the collective consciousness, yet. The fact that there is a return to gardening and growing vegetables, neighbors sharing dinner at home, and vacationing at national parks sends the message that we are trying to connect through the earth, nature, and one another.

I started by searching for my own answers to my slow creeping and mysterious disconnect and recognized much later that this was something worth sharing. I began wondering what I could do to reconnect in a measurable way in my life and to make a difference. I had to find a way to accomplish something quickly and needed tools that could show results immediately. Let's be honest, I was not trying to learn how to build a space shuttle; I just needed a little work on reconnecting.

I began by focusing on one small idea or exercise a week because it is rare that I can set aside an hour a day to quietly meditate, read forty pages of a book, and answer ten questions. That is difficult for almost anybody! I didn't share why or what I was doing with anyone. I just did it for myself. Without any conversation I started to observe friends and clients mimicking the exercises I had done for myself two, three, and four weeks prior. The message received was loud and clear. There were others, like myself, on the path to reconnection. Whether they were choosing this consciously or subconsciously, it didn't really matter. I witnessed great change. By observing others I could see the personification to the power of change and connection. The realization is that we are ready to shift.

While writing this book, I imagined how it would be to simultaneously shift hundreds, millions, and even whole continents into easy weekly exercises and experiences of personal and global reconnection. How incredible it would be to focus in mass on one idea, the idea of connection to ourselves and to one another. Think about what connection really means. Imagine shifting the consciousness of the planet together, united as a whole.

I often got feedback from both clients and friends that I should write a book. I would laugh it off and keep the conversation moving, but as I continued to watch the chasm of the great disconnect, I realized that these simple tools would be helpful to anyone who is ready. You are here and you are ready!

How to Use This Book

∙∙∙∙∙∙∙∙∙∙∙∙∙∙∙∙∙∙∙∙∙∙∙∙∙∙

Change is about having intent and acting on it. That's it.

You will be best served by this book if you view it as guidance and not structure for your life. Do what you can; if you miss a week it is okay, as nothing immediately ties together. Yet, as in life—everything ties together. This is not about feeling guilt or shame about what you haven't done; this is about inner connectedness to yourself and others! What matters now is where you are going and your state of connection when you arrive.

Very little time is needed to read each week's message. The exercises do not need to take a lot of time either. It's more about being in your zone of connection on a daily basis without a huge list of to-do's. The concept is to stick with the same mind-set and exercise for the entire week. You may spend thirty seconds, ten minutes, or an hour; it is your choice. And it is okay to have that amount of time change weekly.

Consciously Connecting is divided into the twelve months of the year; each month corresponds to a theme and contains four weekly lessons. The first chapter starts with January for the sake of monthly continuity; however, you can start this book on any month or week you choose. The framework of each month is to focus on one goal with the idea of moving toward a deeper connection to your inner self.

Each new week begins on a Sunday as there are always four Sundays in a month. There will be a couple of extra days either at the beginning or the end of each month and those days should be used for rest, reflection, fun, or just nothing as you prepare for the next month. Also, don't feel locked into starting your week on a Sunday. If you prefer Tuesday, go with Tuesdays. If you have obligations for the next three Sundays, start on Monday. It's your journey and the sooner you realize this belongs to you, the quicker the essence of your power will be reflected in your choices. The goal is to incorporate the ideas from this book into your daily life, reclaiming what you need most for your reconnection.

Many of the weeks will have stories and examples that link into my life and the two people I share most of my time with: my mom and my husband. Here's a little background:

My mom's name is Pearl and the name fits. She is truly a gem! Born and raised in Chicago during the Depression and divorced when it was considered second to leprosy, she has good midwestern values: work hard, tell the truth, and treat others with kindness and respect. To the mix she adds follow your dreams (however crazy), listen to the voice deep inside (it is always right), and live every day by loving and laughing. Mom took flying lessons when women were barely allowed careers. She consistently got lost driving us anywhere, which in turn made us late to everything, but she always confidently assured my brother and me it was about the journey—not the destination. Mom wore her saddle shoes when no one else did (embarrassing) and took them off when everyone else put them on. She is strong and confident; that's my mom.

My husband, Wayne, entered this world in Texas, and

while he may not have lived there for long, he is still part cowboy! Abandoned as a young child and having lived in an orphanage, he learned to navigate the world without fear. When we met, he rode a Harley, had a ponytail, listened to Garth Brooks, and wore cowboy boots. These days he wears Timberlands, has short hair, but still listens to Garth Brooks. He is unapologetically himself with the perfect balance of strength and tenderness. After his move to New York City, my mom injured her shoulder, and we spent two weeks back in Denver assisting her on the road to recovery. During that time Wayne did some laundry and was unclear about what to do with my mom's underwear. "Wash them," I replied, and so he did. This sort of bonding wasn't what he had in mind!

These are the two people I am most plugged into and continue working to further the depth of our connections. By practicing these exercises you will begin to deepen your connection to the outside world and others. Through connection you become more aligned to your joy, generosity, and spirituality. An inordinate amount of time is spent looking for approval from the outside world desperate for the great external sources of so-called validation. In the midst of that disconnection you have forgotten to look within; you have forgotten to trust yourself. This work is about engaging your focus back onto you—not onto the ego, as there is plenty of that, but the deeper connection.

There seems to be a loss of focus and direction, so it's time to take out your compass and head due north. The answers and the secrets all lie within, waiting for you to tap into your magic. Your awakening to further connection may be as silent as snow falling in the mountains or it may howl like the wind rattling the trees. Reconnecting may be like booming thunder with pockets of lightning burning through the sky. It doesn't matter how you light up, charge up, and sync in. It only matters that you are ignited and ready to tune into your connection and begin this journey. You are about to experience a wonderful adventure as your path of deeper connection and the simple steps to get there await you. Acknowledge this moment and your openness to move out of the abyss of disconnection.

Welcome. Enter here!

JANUARY
Commencement
on Reflection
. . . .

Vow to view January in a new way this year. While this month can be filled with the pressure to start over, begin again, and create lots of new beginnings, laugh at how you have put too much heaviness on yourself in the past, and look at this month with fresh eyes. Year after year it is easy to bite the same hook because you have been programmed to look at January with a specific mind-set. Step away from seeing January as the only time of year to have new beginnings and something great. Understand that something new and something great happen every day, January included, if you are willing to be open and accessible. The truth is that new beginnings and starting over happen when you wake up, with every new project, and in every moment you choose to look at things differently. As you connect deeper within, you begin to realize those are your moments; those are your beginnings.

You may have just fallen from the pedestal of countless unmet, unrealistic expectations, often referred to as the post-holiday crash. Okay, you're still here. Revisit the amusing ways you have put added pressure on yourself all in the name of *January*, which you know from experience usually starts right away on January 1. No time is wasted as you berate yourself for a lack of motivation, your current pant size, and the realization that you have just consumed more sugar than the country of Andorra produces in an entire year. A few extra pounds, a couple of zits—all right, not life threatening. As the calendar turns to January it is easy to move right into the next adventure—judgment.

More than likely every new year you implement a strategic plan to start a new diet and exercise program, and think that every problem in your life will be solved when you cut out all sugar, alcohol, meat, dairy, carbs, and do a juice fast. You are so invigorated you drive by a gym to feel the sweat in the air and convince yourself that the pounds are melting away. Or you could just Google the word *gym* because Google searches are workouts and can be very tiring.

If you belong to a gym you may find yourself raising the bar by doing extra classes, weights, and cardio and nearly killing yourself. Who cares if you can't walk for a week; this is necessary in order to squeeze back into the pants you could wear in October. October of what year? Well that's not for certain, however you will swear that it was last year, sure.

As you have just finished the last holiday marathon of food, frenzy and fun, and are experiencing less daylight, you are probably exhausted and feel more like a bear and want to hibernate. Give yourself permission to hunker down in your cave as you prepare to connect to January in a new and different way! Bears hibernate and it is okay if you want to do a bit of that too. It makes perfect sense not to have the mojo and motivation that will move you in the direction to start a new exercise routine. After all, your body isn't necessarily in sync with the calendar.

Connect mentally to a new program for January because before you can start tuning up your body, you have to start tuning up and connecting to your mind.

Happy new you! Time to get started!

First Sunday in January: Reflect on Slowing Down

So often you may be rushing to get from one place to the next completely unaware of the need to slow down. It is all too easy to get involved with a myriad of lists for projects that need to be completed at home or work, friends you need to call, and all the other infinite things that should be accomplished by Tuesday—of last week. There comes a point where life cannot be just one big checklist you are rushing to finish.

I lovingly call Wayne "turtle" because he is so slow. At any given time I can be five or eight feet ahead of him while doing errands. His reason for moving slower is that it gives him time for something unexpected or to discover something new. His argument is compelling. By hurrying errands we miss out on many discoveries by moving so quickly. From his viewpoint we can do a mix of chores while uncovering unintended, unexpected treasures.

January is the perfect time to slow down and reassess how to move through this year at a calmer and more relaxed pace. Use this week to reevaluate where you want to redirect your energy. It takes courage to redefine, or possibly define for the first time, what your boundaries need to be in order to slow the pace down and step off the spinning merry-go-round. It is common to feel that if you slow down the world will stop. But give it a try.

When I was little I had pregnant guppies in a fishbowl. One evening as my non-aquatic family was heading to a football game, I strolled over to the fishbowl only to discover a baby guppy swimming in the water. Since guppies eat their babies, we had no choice but to wait it out. We found ourselves immersed in the joy and fascination of guppy birth for the next forty-five minutes. We were forced to slow down and arrived late to the game, but we had truly enjoyed the surprise of the moment. There are great gifts and experiences to be had if you let yourself slow down.

This week reflect on areas where you need to slow down and make the commitment to do so. As you find yourself rushing through every task at hand, choose to put on the brakes. Allow for one quality phone call to a friend instead of rushing through four calls that don't have much content but hurriedly get the job done. Maybe you'll opt to enjoy a sunset—the whole sunset and not just one minute—or connect to preparing a meal and focusing on the nourishment it provides.

Acknowledge that when you try to fit too many things into a day, you are missing out on something: your life. Work on connecting to the project, the journey, the moment, and not the end result, which will arrive regardless of the speed chosen. Time doesn't move any quicker just because you do. When you slow down you are more connected and in sync, and as a result you can easily connect to the gifts waiting that may otherwise speed right by!

You do not have to run all the time. Give yourself permission to take a stroll. See you next week.

Second Sunday in January: Reflect Your Blessings

Flush the toxins out of your mind, no greens required. Often it is easier to focus and connect to what you don't have or didn't get for the holidays, forgetting to focus on what you have right now. Gratitude works like a Ferris wheel. The more you focus and connect to your blessings by giving voice to what you are grateful for, the happier the ride and the more abundantly blessings will arrive in your life. The wheel continues to go around and around. Connecting and peering through a lens of gratitude will allow you to see new beginnings, know the road to choose, celebrate your milestones, and realize there is so much more to come.

Think back to your childhood and your nighttime rituals. I would usually get up long after my mom had put me to bed and take all my dolls and stuffed animals out of the closet and place them in bed with me. I would talk to them and share my gratitude that a favorite teacher picked me to carry a note to the main office that day. Or I might talk about how happy I felt due to my success at two square and how much I loved climbing trees and finding caterpillars. Chances are you also practiced gratitude during your childhood in one form or another. However, as you have gotten older, you may have disconnected from the link.

In truth, it is easy to find a little time to connect to gratitude and give thanks for the many blessings in your life. The form—whether through prayer, inner monologue while driving, or using a journal—is not the important piece. What is important is that you choose to do this in the way that resonates for you. The journey to greater abundance is slowed and sometimes stalled when voice of gratitude is not given to your existing blessings.

There are two parts to your journey this week. The first idea is about adjusting your internal gratitude dialogue, as well as the dialogue you share with others. Each time you catch yourself verbalizing what you do not want in your life, work to change the imprint of your thoughts toward gratitude. Today you begin laying the groundwork for tomorrow.

If the dialogue of the moment is about how much you dislike your job, work on shifting into the place of gratitude. Put some power to the words as you recognize this job gives you the ability to live your current lifestyle. This job also allows you to work toward your goal, the goal of a new job.

If you don't like your home, change the verbiage to how thankful and grateful you are to have a place to live. Acknowledge that you are grateful for new opportunities, which, when ready, will reveal themselves toward receiving the blessing of a new home. The idea is to catch yourself in the moments when you are not coming from a place of gratitude and replace the negative dialogue with what you are grateful for today. Always be cognizant that you are open to moving your life into the next realm of what you would like your reality to become as you choose and use words more carefully. As my mom steadfastly reminds me, "Thoughts are things and words are powerful tools."

The second piece for the week is a small list of five things that allow you to feel gratitude. Before rising each morning or maybe in the shower and before falling asleep each evening, go through your list and give thanks. If this feels difficult, look to the obvious. Give thanks for having two eyes that can see or glasses to help correct your vision, two legs that allow you to walk or a wheelchair that gets you where you need to go. Maybe you are grateful for your car, a good breakfast, a job interview, friends, or the new tech device. Give thanks for five blessings twice each day for all seven days. The five items on your list can change daily, but the minimum is five.

I'm grateful you see the value in connecting. See you next week.

Third Sunday in January: Reflect on the Holidays

Take some time to digest and evaluate what did and did not work during the last holiday season. Begin by thinking about your holidays, what you connected to versus what you did not. What would you hope or wish to do differently if those few weeks were a blank slate? Often there are activities that don't feel like a fit or make you uncomfortable, thus giving you desire to make a change. Start envisioning what you hope to change and do differently this year.

Is it overspending, which is easy to do and can leave you bogged down by debt for the next ten months? If so, it may be time to draw names for gifts and set a realistic per person spending limit. Maybe indulging in too much food and partying requires you to set some new limitations. Or it could be a lot of bickering or other behavior that is sabotaging a better plan. This year you will take charge of your holiday season and create exactly what you would like to experience. This doesn't mean you don't love the traditions your family has created or that you don't respect your in-laws. A blank slate simply means you need to find your truth and what resonates with you so the connection can be made.

What are the five things you would like to do with reference to the holidays this coming year? Possibly you and a loved one need to go away just the two of you, for some quiet time, connecting, and reflecting. Don't allow guilt to interfere with the freedom to make the decision that will work best in your life. If you would like to have Thanksgiving dinner at a restaurant this year—no muss, no fuss—then plan it. It is easy to create the holidays that you would like to have, but you must first decide what you would like.

One year I had Thanksgiving with friends who did not like turkey. Those seven people liked chicken casserole, so that is what they cooked, instead of turkey. This family clearly embraced their holiday to fit what they wanted and not what is dictated as the ideal Thanksgiving meal. Maybe you prefer fish or filet mignon. Once you realize that the holidays are really about the unity with one another and the connection you find within yourself, it won't matter what is on the plate or where the meal is served.

Allow yourself to connect into the evolution of your truth. From that path you will radiate the true meaning of the holidays by coming together with family, friends, and, most importantly, yourself. Take the first five days this week to make your list. You will then have two days to ponder, tweak, and adjust the plan. Place this piece of paper in an envelope, and then seal it and tuck it away in a drawer for safekeeping. Make a note where you put it so you can open it the second week of November. As the year rolls by and the holiday season approaches, you will have your plan of action ready for execution.

Unveil the possibility of new ideas and traditions. See you next week.

Fourth Sunday in January: Reflect on Unsubscribing

Take a moment to think about how many emails you receive in one day and how often you open your inbox and groan. How quickly it is encumbered by another twenty-five, forty, or seventy new emails that seem to need immediate attention. Or so you think. But more importantly than that, you have signed up for emails that are not needed, yet you have difficulty hitting unsubscribe.

Make the choice to be as selective about your inbox as you are when choosing a new friend. All right, not quite, but you get the point. Signing up for everything so you miss nothing not only wastes your time but also causes undue stress. Guard your precious time and create an inbox that holds something you are really interested in and information you need.

If you're receiving weekly coupons from a store that is no longer compatible with your sense of style, unsubscribe. Do you receive emails from numerous travel sites yet you do not have the money for or interest in travel? Unsubscribe. If you get email blasts from catalogue companies from which you have never purchased anything, you know what to do. If you haven't booked a spa service, sporting event, concert, or anything else from that site, *un-sub-scribe*. If signing up for investment sites, horoscopes, vitamins, or wholesale housewares cause you to groan and think, *Not this again*, it's time to do yourself a favor and unsubscribe.

You will still be informed on the newest, latest, and best of everything as information will always circulate in your direction. Whether through the news, friends, or coworkers, if you are meant to know something, the information will find you. There is no need to suffer through daily inbox clutter when all you have to do is unsubscribe.

Start now to lessen your load by unsubscribing to the emails encumbering you and keeping you tethered to your device. There is no need to hoard them in a pending file in an attempt to tidy up your inbox. If the junk drawer has too much junk, you start tossing things out, permanently. It's the same principle here. The next seven days will help you reclaim some of your free time, more tranquility, and the connection of what should really be in your inbox: messages from friends and family, favorite stores, and book club suggestions. Unsubscribe to a minimum of one unnecessary email per day.

Unsubscribe, but not here. See you next week.

FEBRUARY
Love Yourself More, XO!
....

February is the month associated with love and romance, so start working on the connection to loving the most important person in your life—*you!* A couple of years ago Wayne and I were in Vietnam on Valentine's Day. The sidewalks were covered with flowers and heart-shaped candy boxes in different sizes. We found this to be curious since Valentine's Day is largely an American holiday, and we wondered why they were celebrating in Vietnam. One of our waiters explained that the young people of Vietnam want to love and to be loved, so they have started celebrating this wonderful American expression of love. Many of the Vietnamese have become enamored with this tradition in a very short time.

Beautiful, red, heart-shaped boxes of candy and flowers are wonderful to receive, but they cannot fill the emptiness if you don't first feel the connection of love to yourself. First, you must learn to love the most important person on this journey: *you*. As you stamp the seal of approval upon yourself and connect at your deepest core, you realize this will bring more hearts and flowers than you ever imagined and disguised in ways you never dreamed.

First Sunday in February: Love Your Inner Voice

Begin this week by recognizing the need to disconnect from the all-too-familiar, negative, demeaning, belittling inner voice. The critical voice pointing out the mistakes you have made in life, the voice that is quick to judge and softly whispers how your life is a mess and there are no other options. Back up and erase, as that is a complete untruth! When your inner dialogue speaks critically and negatively, it disconnects you from your supportive voice and undermines your process to succeed and move forward in a productive and creative life.

This week when the negative, critical, and undermining voice starts talking, allow this to be an opportunity of awareness of the spiritual undermining and make a conscious choice to put on the brakes. Stop. Work to recognize this internal dialogue, cease the internal chatter, and replace the harsh words with positive and reaffirming statements.

This may feel awkward and be difficult, especially if you have had this internal dialogue for most of your life. Regardless, your job this week is to replace this negativity with the polar opposite. The positive mantra now becomes "I am making the best choices I can in the present moment and every moment of my awareness." If you keep telling yourself that you have made poor choices in life, instead remind yourself that you are on a journey. Every choice you have made is a piece of the fabric of you. The fabric comes in a myriad of sizes, shapes, and colors, and no one piece is wrong or doesn't fit. Cease the urge to continually pull and tug at the lose threads, as you do not want the cloth to unravel. Begin to accept that these uneven and unfinished threads are part of the whole quilt, the patchwork of your life story. Work to finish the stitches and close off the loose ends, which can only be done by moving forward, not by going back.

The constant replaying of dialogue condemning the past keeps you frozen and disconnected from your truth. Often, time is spent looking back and daydreaming about having another chance to do something differently and, of course, doing it better. But this does not propel you forward or connect you into your greatness and your untapped talent. Hear this at your core: you would not have done anything differently. The yesterday you is not who you are today. You are able to assess things differently today because you are wiser after connecting to the pitfalls of yesterday. You are mentally and spiritually stronger today, which allows you to see all the other possibilities that didn't exist before. Understand the relevance your past has to the fabric of your today; acknowledge the gifts, however painful; and adjust your thinking and dialogue to support the wonder that awaits as something new begins today!

Spend this week cognizant of the tone of your inner voice. Modify the message of your inner voice, and latch onto the knowledge that words are powerful and you will use the power to your good. Listen closely to the chant confirming how much progress you have made in life, how great you are at your job, how loyal you are as a friend, how well you honor your path of spirituality, and all the other wonderful pieces of your fabric. Move like a race-car driver; cut the negativity off when it tries to enter your lane, speed up, and fill up with the good stuff.

Listen carefully and chant the praises. See you next week.

Second Sunday in February: Love Your Body

As a society we have become unnecessarily critical of our bodies and seem to have lost good judgment when it comes to labeling people as fat and obese. These overused and false descriptions (used mostly by women) grant permission to continue berating oneself as well as others. No one can deny we have an epidemic of overweight people in our country; however, the misuse of the word *fat* is one more way to use ourselves as a punching bag for everything that is frustrating. As the dial is turned up on connecting to your positive inner voice and giving attention to what you love—yes, *love*— about yourself, you are able to bring more love energy into your life. Start purposefully navigating your course, paying careful attention to how you expend your energy and for what purpose.

Have you ever followed advice from the magazine articles that instruct you to find a picture of your ideal body in a magazine, cut it out, and then attach a photo of your head to the picture? Usually that picture is to be placed on a mirror, refrigerator, or some other location in your home that you pass by often, so it can inspire and motivate you to have the body you want. Many decades ago I tried that experiment, and each time I looked at the photo, I thought of the model and never really saw myself. This is an odd exercise, as someone who is 5'1" will never have Heidi Klum's legs no matter how much visualization or arts and crafts exercises are done.

However, you have at least one photo that makes you feel good about your body, and you love what you look like in that special photo. Your photo might be from a favorite vacation or from a friend's wedding, maybe your own wedding.

Regardless of the photograph, you know which picture makes you smile and feel good on the inside. Chances are your eyes are sparkling, your smile is genuine and beaming, and your body is relaxed, irrespective of your dress or pant size. This photo is powerful as it contains the essence of the real you—the you who is loved unconditionally and is free from the internal chatter keeping you from loving that very body today.

Begin this week by finding a photo that will connect you to appreciating all the gifts your body brings to you daily. Take a day or two to find that photo, if you don't have it already, and put the photo on your mirror, nightstand, anywhere it can be viewed numerous times each day. Scan the photo and make it the background or lock screen on your phone, computer, and tablet.

During the week test your gauge of acceptance with the love you have for your body exactly as it is today. Find a minimum of three things you love about your body; reconfirm and recommit to what makes your body so amazing. Possibly it's a great smile, teeth that are straight, a great bottom, tight abs, thick and luscious hair, pretty feet, or shoulders that fit your body perfectly. What do you love about your body? What do people compliment you on? There will be conflicting thoughts of negativity that creep into your mind, that's okay. Acknowledge them, dismiss the negativity, and move on.

This is about connecting and giving energy to what you love rather than what you don't. Understand this is not a magic fix and one week will not change years of the other stuff. But one change of habit gives way to help change something else that no longer fits your life, allowing and beginning a shift in your consciousness. Tuning into your energy is a connection worth making. Consciously become aware of how energy can be scattered and wasted focusing on issues that do not propel you toward your good or what you deserve; that is a true disconnection from the self. Shifting energy and refocusing to what is great will clear the path for the rest. This is about nurturing seedlings, not looking for an eight-foot sunflower in bloom.

For each of the remaining days in the week the protocol is fairly easy. Each time you see the photo take a moment to acknowledge that picture and how it makes you feel. Verbally and consciously remind yourself that this is the body you love, and think of the three things that you really, really love. Own it and bask in it; this is your truly amazing body.

Keep the photo with your own head on your own body. See you next week!

Third Sunday in February: Love the Disconnect

I am guilty of checking my phone when I hear it ping. I gaze around the room and witness others doing the same. A few years back Wayne and I visited Aruba, leaving our cell phones and computers at home. We were amazed to see almost everyone on the beach and at the pool with their phones and tablets in hand. Going to the beach for us was about swimming, relaxing, and snorkeling. The last thing we wanted was to connect with the outside world. We were working on the connection to ourselves and each other.

If you feel the need to stay 100 percent connected to the office and ongoing projects back home, you might as well save your hard-earned money and your flight miles. Put away the suntan lotion, stay home, and stick with the routine because you have not unplugged and disconnected one bit. The only difference would be sitting in a lounge chair as opposed to an office chair and drinking something with an umbrella in it instead of the usual iced coffee. Nothing would have changed in your routine except your location.

The more you technologically connect, the less you connect to yourself and others. Ask yourself, "What is so important that it cannot wait?" Look, if the terror threat has just escalated to red and the CIA is alerting you, by all means keep your phone handy and tell me too, but seriously. How about getting your retail therapy from local shops as opposed to shopping on your device poolside? The old adage of there is a time and a place for everything still applies.

Wayne and I live in New York City, and we often attend the theater. I am fascinated watching people and their varying behaviors. Before we were tethered to our cell phones

24-7, theater etiquette was very different, especially during intermission. I rarely see audience members discussing the play or musical anymore, but I often see people immediately disconnect from the experience to enter the communion to technology. The cell phones come out, and schedules are planned. I witness rapid fingers responding to emails, but very little, if any, conversation about the theater experience.

This week disconnect from all those wonderful devices. When meeting friends for dinner, place your phone on vibrate and in your pocket, not on the corner of the table. Shut the phone off when you enter the movie theater, and do not turn it on until you leave. And by the way, turning it off is different from vibrate. It can be pretty annoying when Meryl Streep is mastering one more accent and the stranger next to you has a phone that will not stop vibrating!

Numerous acquaintances have told me how they place their cell phones on their nightstand for the sole purpose of checking emails in the wee hours of the morning. Unless you are experiencing extenuating circumstances in your life, this is probably addictive behavior. By disconnecting your filters you allow information to creep into your mind round the clock without taking a rest. Think about this: Would you leave your front door open all day, all night, 24-7, 365 days a year? No, you would not. You go to school, work, church, meetings, and dates, and the front door remains closed. You may not lock it, but at a certain time it closes down for the day. You must do the same with the door to your mind. Close it down to all the jabbering, mindlessness, and consumerism, and allow it time to rest. When your front door is closed, your home is resting and no one can enter without a key or your permission. You must allow your mind to rest as well.

If you are worried about the discipline or willpower needed for this week, then leave your phone at home when you head out to the grocery store or dry cleaner. Leave the phone in the hotel safe and connect to your vacation and not what is happening back home.

When you disconnect, the real connection can begin. See you next week.

Fourth Sunday in February: Love Your Home

Home represents a sanctuary that is safe and calm from the outside world. Every home has at least one area that provides a place for contemplation or gives inspiration. Maybe you like sitting in a special chair while gazing out the window or perhaps you enjoy being tucked away in a corner on a beautiful rug with a few comfy pillows.

I have two favorite areas in my home. The first is sitting on a settee in our bedroom where I enjoy looking out the window at the trees and people passing by on the street below. The other place is in our foyer sitting in my childhood chair, which I recovered in a beautiful deep-red fabric with an elephant print. From here I enjoy gazing on a Buddha, purchased in Thailand, as he keeps watch over our home. The childhood chair connects me spiritually, allowing me to focus while I do some soul searching. The other connects me to my creativity; ideas rush into my head and I quickly devise the next steps of my current project. Sitting in this spot ignites a fire in me that cannot be extinguished and all things become possible.

It's easy to get caught in the trap of focusing on the lack of resources to have the home you would like; however, do not let this become your focus. This is the week to move a chair or rearrange the furniture in a room in order to love your home. If you want to see a favorite picture or painting first thing in the morning, then take it off the living room wall and put in the bedroom. Buy a few colorful pillows for the sofa or maybe a new rug to give a room its facelift. Do what is allowed in your budget and connect to your home by creating the joy, tranquility, and peace you desire.

If you have always wanted to paint the walls in a room, or just one wall for accent, make the commitment, and do it this week. Paint, a brush and roller, covers for your furniture, and desire is all that is required. Go with a color that stirs your soul, awakens your passions, and makes you believe that everything and anything is possible. Maybe you need to take a break from color and devote a space to white, starting new and fresh, with ideas never imagined previously on your blank slate.

Find a piece of furniture, a corner, something that makes you love being in your home and gives you access to the gratitude voice. If the thought of painting a room is too daunting, consider purchasing a new slipcover for a chair, a new lamp, or a few plants, and then let this area be your grounding station. Tap into what changes will allow you to connect to the harmony of your home so your creative muses can safely emerge and do what they do best—inspire. Enter into your inner sanctum both in your home and yourself by spending some time in this place after you have made it what you want.

Make the change, create, and connect to your ideal domain. See you next week.

MARCH

Spring into Action

....

Congratulate yourself as you continue to connect with the work or as you begin your commitment now; either way you are here! Daylight saving time will arrive this month and you welcome spring. While everything outside is reemerging with freshness and life, you are too. Attitudes start to shift, so you start to shift as well. As you leave work to pick up the kids or run errands in the evening, you begin to feel lighter since there is more daylight to do these chores. You arrive home feeling more refreshed and ready to embrace the next set of tasks in the kitchen or as you help with homework, pay the bills, or finish your workday.

Just like bears emerging from hibernation, you have the desire to do more for yourself without feeling the drain of winter. As you delve deeper into the conscious choices of the food you put into your body and learn to feel the impact, you are opening yourself to the whole body-mind connection. This is the month to start exercising your body (if you aren't already doing so), as you are ready. There is no competing with movie stars or models. You are here to connect into the gratitude of what your body can do and your physical well-being. Working out with a friend and motivating one another is a great way to commit; however, do not buy into the sabotage and cruelty of not having the body of someone else. You continue the work to love your body and have the picture on your lock screen to prove it (see "Second Sunday in February: Love Your Body")! This path is the springboard leading you out of viperous territory as you continue to work to erase old patterns of thinking and continue to move in the direction of your truth.

Wishing to be another person is an unrealistic fantasy.

Working to emulate something you admire needs to be based in the reality that you are unique and a mirror image to no one. While it is fine to appreciate the toned stomach or arms of another (and use it as motivation), recognize the tools that will help you attain these goals and be grounded in the reality that you can never acquire those identical arms, as they belong to someone else. The understanding that your body is one of a kind connects into freedom and the acceptance of your truth. Steer your inner voice to be sure it knows the beauty and strength of your body and work with the goal of making your body better.

First Sunday in March: Spring into Movement

This week commit and connect to understanding your tolerance for exercising your physical body. Your work to break through so many barriers and limiting ideas will allow further connection into your physical body. The beautiful body never gives up, never says no, and keeps transporting you daily, so it is time to show your body some love and gratitude. Explore how you can push the limits while always being respectful of the information your body shares with you as you continue to fine-tune the art of listening.

If there hasn't been any physical exercise in your life whatsoever, you can start by walking. Your financial status doesn't matter, as the only cost is your commitment. Remember, this is part of the journey to your reconnection, and part of your connection is not running out of breath after one flight of stairs or when flipping steaks on the barbeque. If you have been consistently working out, start to test your limits and your endurance, and push to give a little more to the workout.

If you live in a part of the world where driving is required, adjust your thinking when it comes to parking. Try something new when you go to the mall, grocery store, work, or any location with a parking lot. Park as far out as you possibly can in the last and least desirable spot. Use your good judgment and don't do this if you are alone late at night. Can you imagine the crush of the holiday season and how parking lots would look if every driver was looking for the parking space farthest from a store? These spots would become the prime and sought-after parking areas, which is really funny when you think about it.

If you don't drive but rather live in a big metropolitan city, alter how you commute. Do not go to the bus or subway stop nearest to your home or work; instead walk to the next station or skip two stations. Listen to your body. If this seems impossible because you live in a rainy area, make sure you take an umbrella if rain is in the forecast. Be cautious of buying into the excuses you may be generating right now.

Walking is such great exercise. It is easy on the knees, gets your heart rate up, is great for weight loss, and does not demand anything from your budget since it is free. No excuses, right? Wayne and I used to live on the eleventh floor and we would often walk up the stairs to our apartment. Sometimes we would even race each other and I usually won! Although that would depend on whom you ask, but since this is my book, I usually won. Joking aside, this was a great way to get some exercise without having to spend money and join a gym.

While walking, live in the moment. Feel the connection to your surroundings and the ground beneath your feet. It is easy to take walking for granted, so tune into your gratitude, and live in the moment of this gift. This type of walking is your exercise, so silence your cell phone, or use it exclusively to listen to motivating music. If listening to music you must resist the temptation to answer any phone calls or texts or check emails while engaged in your workout. You might kick and scream at the idea, but this time is for you. Connect to the moment of being. Look up at the world while digesting all the beauty that surrounds you, which you may be noticing for the first time. If you can walk in a park, notice the beauty of the trees blossoming and coming to life after hibernating for the winter. Look up to the beautiful blue sky with the bright sun or maybe it's a darker sky with magic and mystery. It all reconnects you back to nature. If you are in a city the walk is different but no less enchanting. Look at the varying styles of architecture, which can be fascinating, and the silliness of how similarly dogs and their owners mirror one another in looks. Bask in the beauty of so many different nationalities sharing one common space harmoniously as you realize your great fortune to be part of this majestic fabric. Appreciate it. Vocalize some gratitude.

If exercise is a difficult concept let this be the door that now opens. Commit to this all the way and be persistent. Incorporate this into your life by making it a priority. Understand you are feeding your mind-body connection and the spirit-body connection. There are easy and inexpensive ways to work exercise into your schedule. Find that buddy to walk with at lunch or after work. If your schedule is tight, take the stairs at work or during your lunch break. Think outside the box and be creative if you are afraid to try a class at a gym or cannot afford to. This week begin your commitment to fifteen minutes a day, and if you have been exercising all along, add an extra fifteen minutes to your routine.

Release yourself to your body. See you next week.

Second Sunday in March: Spring into Freedom

It probably isn't too often, if ever, that you feel free enough to dance alone or sing out loud full throttle, a rock star holding the hair brush—you know what I'm talking about. A personal favorite activity is talking to myself. While you may not do this, it can be quite useful as some of the best answers lie within. A conversation like this may offer answers to questions and problems lying deep and dormant. Set the scene as if chatting with a boss, family member, television interviewer, or any other source. Your imagination is freed and open to limitless possibilities for problem solving. Your inner monologue helps you gain clarity as it stops the spinning in your head and allows you to hear and feel things differently.

Wayne loves to come home and quietly enter our house only to find me in the kitchen talking to myself. He can only listen for two to four minutes until he starts giggling and wondering who I am conversing with and about what. I have talked to myself my entire life, and in truth I have found more solutions to problems than not. It is therapy for working out difficult or puzzling situations. As I was writing this book, you could have seen me at any time walking the streets of New York City talking to myself—translation: working on this book.

This liberated release is no different from dancing with yourself, which Wayne loves to do when given the chance. Payback allows me to find him dusting or vacuuming the living room in his underwear, dancing as if he is about to go on tour with Beyoncé. I try to stave off the laughter for as long as possible, also without much success.

Whether you want to dance, talk to yourself, enjoy walking through puddles, or participate in any other sort of behavior considered somewhat crazy to do alone or as an adult, this is your week to begin. Tap into the secret place deep inside of you that harbors the creative juices, and let that kid who doesn't care what the world thinks spring free. As you continue to exercise, sing a song out loud, talk to yourself, or engage in the freedom to boogie as you take your evening stroll and begin connecting to the freer spirit. It's like the title to Pharoah Sanders's song "You've Got to Have Freedom."

Free yourself and enjoy it. See you next week.

Third Sunday in March: Spring into Health

As you move forward with new tasks at hand and new ways to explore your life, the commitment is to continuously engage your body in some kind of daily exercise and movement. Taking the stairs twice a day or continuing your evening walk are great options to stay in sync with this part of your connection.

This week take a look at what foods you consume and how you can fine-tune those choices for more energy to your brain and body. One reason for overeating is not connecting to the food and/or the company while dining. By eating quickly and staying engaged to your devices, the connection of food to the brain, doesn't register until much later, and at that point you may be looking for more food. Trying to get sated by eating on the run results in disconnect from the intimacy of the taste and smell of a delicious meal and leaves you craving something else.

Observe how much caffeine you consume each day or how often you eat fast food. Examine and focus on what you are putting into your body. It is easy to be critical and dissatisfied with your food choices, but try to remove the criticism and focus on the positive. Commit to making one small change: give up the morning donut, pack a lunch to control fat intake, or choose to set aside thirty minutes at night to cook a healthful and nutritious dinner. These are steps to a better lifestyle that will aid in giving you more energy and bringing optimal benefits to your health.

Where are you willing to cut the fat, no pun intended, so you can rev up your body and brain to their fullest daily potential? This doesn't translate into never having your favorite coffee drink again, but maybe once a week is enough for your health and your wallet. Start to veer away from junk foods and their massive amounts of salt, sugar, and fats, and substitute fruit instead. You will find your body starts to crave the natural sugar that an apple provides. You will also be amazed at how delicious vegetables and fruit begin to taste as your taste buds become more awakened and alive. Many of the foods that are not the best choices dull the taste buds and slow down your brain. Begin to transition away from these foods and you will notice an increase in your physical well-being and the enjoyment you feel as you continue to move and stay active.

This is the third week in the third month of the calendar and it is about three choices that will allow you to further connect into your well-being.

- Choose three foods to cut out or cut down on. (Soda pop, potato chips, candy bars?)
- Strategize and implement three ways to change your meals to assist in your weight and life goals. (Add more vegetables and fruit or consume fewer carbs, meat, or cheese?)
- Analyze three trigger foods that send you into orbit by setting off the cycle of cravings. Commit to eating these foods less often, as they are not working in harmony with your body.

Maybe you need to cut out the afternoon snack of junk food and replace it with a banana or some of those cute baby carrots. Do you need to start substituting water for everything else that you are drinking during the day? Maybe you already drink water but need to increase the amount you drink to help stave off those hunger pangs that drive you to the vending machines. Once you are open to awareness, the change has already begun!

Connect to your food source. See you next week.

Fourth Sunday in March: Spring into Giving

As you begin to feel unencumbered from the winter and continue connecting with the beauty of spring, look within to become a leader for those who are less fortunate and may need a helping hand. As you give to yourself, follow the trail of giving to others as well. Recognize there will always be those who have more and those who have less. This is the week to connect with those who are in need.

When I was in elementary school, twice a year (like clockwork) my mom would ask my brother and me to choose ten toys or books that we were no longer using and we would head off to a home for underprivileged kids. She would explain the importance of giving to those who had less and the need to connect to these kids by showing them love from the outside world. We would spend the day reading stories and playing with the kids, and on the drive home we would relive the joys of the day.

As would be expected, we did not give up our toys without an argument, but we learned the value of connecting to those who needed some help. What you focus on this week will be uplifting as you further your connection to people who have not mastered the journey in the same way. You may want to serve a meal at a shelter, allowing others to feel cared for and encouraged, or you may want to start collecting canned goods at your church, allowing the spirit of giving to multiply as many quickly choose to help. Invite your elderly neighbor over for dinner, give your old sweater or gloves to a homeless person, volunteer time at your favorite museum, or volunteer to read books to children at the local library. There are so many options for giving that do not require a financial commitment. If you can afford to write a check to an individual or an organization that needs help, then this is the week to get out your pen and proceed. But if money is tight, be creative as you connect to this part of your life. Give time, give money, or both. Connect!

This week the goal is to give one act of kindness and generosity to someone every day. Allow this to help you think outside the box: a warm smile to a grocery clerk, holding the door for someone, or visiting a nursing home where a smiling face would be welcomed. Offer to pick up medicine for a sick friend or give a neighbor a ride to the airport. If a coworker is struggling with Excel spreadsheets, offer to help and share some of your knowledge. Take the challenge and do this for all seven days as you see the plethora of opportunities around every corner and continue connecting to giving in the days and weeks to follow. This is about giving without the expectation of receiving something in return. Remember the story of the Grinch: once he understood the gift of giving, his heart grew three times in size.

By giving to others you give to yourself. See you next week.

APRIL

Connecting the Dots

· ·

This month you'll begin reprogramming new thoughts on some old, familiar ideas. When you bridge an old concept with a new plan of action, you'll feel your power on a deeper level, and that connection is the answer to getting a real power surge.

First Sunday in April: Connect to Friendship

This week reflect and put the spotlight on friendship. Allowing for a deeper connection to friends as you realize what and who is already working in your life. Look at your inner circle; you know who always has your back. These people will meet you at the emergency room at two in the morning, hold your hand at a funeral, and laugh with you about all the challenges catapulted in your direction. These are the people you are grateful to have in your life.

Friends and family who are connected with you at the deepest level are wonderful gifts. They nourish your soul. These individuals are your treasures and this week you'll place them center stage and focus on these relationships. Choose one person who understands what you are all about and consistently offers support and encouragement. Allocate time this week for an outing or other form of connection with this significant person in your life. Allowing your soul to be nurtured continues the quest to surpassing what you thought was possible and enables you to enter a new understanding of the impossibly possible. If your encouraging friend or family member lives three thousand miles away, then make a phone date to catch up. However, if distance does not pose a problem, meet for a walk in the park or go to the mountains or the shore. Take time to share with and listen to this person as you continue to deepen your connection not only to yourself but to another as well.

It is easy to forget how important it is to listen as opposed to verbalizing all your thoughts and the questions you need answered. My mom has always made it a point to say we have only one mouth and two ears for a good reason. Therefore, the listening to talking ratio should always be 2:1. Encourage a friend to share and use this as your opportunity to be a good listener. Listening opens up the potential to view obstacles through a new paradigm while reviewing solutions that were not available prior to listening. Listening also works to open your heart, allowing you to connect to the joy and sorrow of another and thus helping you to strike balance in your life.

Focus on those who cultivate your soul and allow yourself to do the same for them. This week extend yourself beyond the reaches of you and embrace the one, two, or three people who so tenderly and powerfully embrace you.

Encircle yourself with another. See you next week.

Second Sunday in April: Connect to Responsibility

Responsibility is learned in baby steps and often proves to be most challenging in matters of finance. One piece of the puzzle is being able to manage your finances no matter how large or small the number on your bank statement may be. Treating money thoughtfully and with respect will open the path to understanding how money can work for you as opposed to you being its prisoner. You can modify the imprint of how you consider and execute financial obligations if you allow yourself some time to think of the ramifications prior to making the commitment.

It is easy to feel you deserve any trinket desired in the moment and so you may be quick to take out the plastic and purchase. But riding the roller coaster of debt is plagued with sleepless nights and an increase in your level of stress. Consistently having the contingency plan to *charge it* can prove to be a treacherous path with costly lessons ahead. Incurring penalties in interest and late fees that will take months and sometimes years to pay and cost thousands more than anticipated will be agonizing.

The need to feed the hungry consumer has become further entrenched by credit card companies willing to help. Do not misunderstand my feelings about credit cards; there is a time and a place for their use and I am not against them. Credit cards have been helpful and provide added protection for me when renting cars and traveling the world, and I love the points and rewards. The plastic card is not the enemy— the hungry consumer who wants it all is! However, you can learn to do a better job with your financial accountability by choosing to responsibly review what is and is not within your budget.

This week examine where you are disconnected from finances. Have you added all the premium channels to your cable box before consulting your other financial obligations? Are you leasing a fancy car when instead you should be purchasing a smaller used car to fit your budget? Have you opened store credit cards to get an extra 10–15 percent off your first purchase? If so, close out and shred the cards, and don't continue to participate in those deals. It is so tempting to overspend and use those store cards for something that you don't need but are able to justify because you have the card and there is a sale. Instead of buying coffee on the way to work, make it at home and take it with you. How about having ten or fifteen dollars deducted (via direct deposit) from each paycheck and sent to a savings account you have opened? Start thinking about all the ways you are leaking cash. If your car were leaking oil you would get it fixed!

If you are not generating enough income to pay your monthly credit card balance in full, then a current item you are thinking about purchasing is not a wise choice and you need to walk away. No one has ever died or gotten a disease from a lack of shopping. In fact, retailers understand the current economic climate and many have gone back to the option of layaway. By paying something each week until your item is purchased in full you will follow your budget restrictions and better understand the value of your money. This is a great option but only if you can afford to do it!

Consider the option of not using an ATM or debit card and instead take your spending money out of the bank for the week and leave the cards at home. Use your cash until it runs out and then find some other fun that is free. Play a game with yourself to see how many adventures you can have with thirty or forty dollars. By relying on the consistent use of ATM and debit cards, you are all too easily setting yourself up to overspend and pay costly overdraft and ATM fees. To this day I don't have an ATM card, but I always have money in the bank. When my cash is gone, it is time to head home.

You are building a fortress, block by block (as you connect to these exercises each week), and an army (family, friends, and coworkers) to support what you need. This can sometimes take a circuitous route, but you will get there. Make the choice not to be discouraged or shy away as you examine your areas of disconnect. Instead choose to roll up your sleeves and enter uncharted waters.

By working to delay your gratification, you can begin to feel the freedom of living without financial turmoil. It is much easier to get a good night's sleep when you are not worried about how you are going to pay your credit cards or any bill for that matter. Financial responsibility connects to your commitment of maturity and being mature means having the discipline to know the difference between wanting something and needing something. Within that framework you understand the reality of where your finances are today and recognize you are capable and resourceful and can get exactly what you desire in the future. Spend one to two days deciding what your financial accountability issues are and where to put your focus and energy, and then begin.

Do a reality check, and keep moving forward. See you next week.

Third Sunday in April: Connect to Words

It's time to start connecting to your words by empowering the content of your daily dialogue with positive and nonjudgmental verbal communication. How often do you find yourself or others in conversations laced with the insidious tone of criticism? There seem to be countless opinions about people being too fat, wearing unattractive clothing, having weird hair, or being too ethnic (I'm not even sure what that one means), and unfortunately much of this type of verbiage is from women about other women. Criticism about everything sounds like a bad bumper sticker.

Negative thoughts create indelible imprints on your mind that hook into critical and verbally abusive dialogue, furthering disconnect. These types of verbal assaults give a viewpoint that becomes distorted and through time will inextricably become intertwined with the reflection of who you are. Choosing to speak unkindly over and over, day in and day out, shifts what you focus on (which by the way is really nothing more than negativity) and can incorrectly color how you view the world.

Explore these ideas and ask yourself, "Am I on the inside or the outside of this arena?" Be honest. If you have been participating in the office gossip or catch yourself berating others while with friends, make a decision to exit this arena and consciously choose to connect to a kinder path.

You know and understand this is not your truth, as no one arrives on the planet negative and critical. We all arrive wide-eyed, innocent, full of wonder, and open to the adventures of a magical journey. Some have been taught to surrender from the true language of joy and inquisitiveness and have entered into the arena of self-doubt and criticism. If that has been your path, here is the exit sign—come with me. The sign is flashing, it is big and beautiful, and it is your truth. You are going to rewire yourself back to the factory setting.

The next seven days may feel like a month, but you must commit with zeal and forge ahead. If this week is difficult to accomplish, you will realize you have some work to do, as a nerve has been struck. Sometimes that is the best way to achieve a new pattern of behavior. By the way, this isn't a peace, love, and kumbaya exercise trying to stifle your ability to vent if necessary. This is merely a gauge to check the temperature on how and why you vent.

This week if those in your surroundings embark on a tirade of criticism directed at others, you will get up and walk away. This is the best way to stop from indulging and exploiting what can lead to the darker side. If you are in a group setting and cannot dismiss yourself, choose to either disagree, while making the point that this type of conversation is a waste of time or choose to remain silent. Wear a rubber band on your wrist for the week, and each time you find yourself caught up in the gossip and criticism of another, snap the rubber band on your wrist. Believe me: after ten or twenty good snaps you won't want to say anything about anyone! Another option to end this dialogue has to do with money—your money. Each time you gossip or criticize, place one dollar in a jar and at the end of the week donate the money to your favorite charity or organization, and no, you cannot be your favorite charity.

The goal for this week is to avoid mindless gossiping or criticism of others because you understand that feeds a diet of disconnection. Twenty-four hours a day for seven days is the whole week, and it starts now. Follow me to the entrance of a brighter arena that holds the kind words which will allow you to support and inspire everyone. Remember, the person who greets you daily in the mirror will look exactly how you are on the inside!

Reset and rewire. See you next week.

Fourth Sunday in April: Connect to Others

It is interesting and fun to test how connected you are to the people you interact with each day. Get into an elevator with a complete group of strangers and try to make eye contact or share a basic hello. This might be doable provided everyone isn't on his or her phone. However, you may be surprised when people momentarily look up and avoid eye contact. When Wayne thinks he is in trouble for some forgotten chore, the joke in our house is to avoid eye contact. Of course we laugh about this every time he does it; however it could be most people have come to believe this. Or they were raised by a pack of raccoons. It's hard to say.

As a child I was taught to say hello to my neighbors when I went outside. Not doing so was considered rude. Back in the day we also greeted bank tellers and grocery clerks. When I went for walks with my mom or grandmother, we would also acknowledge those we passed on the sidewalk. When I first moved to New York City I was so offended that no one would give me any sort of greeting on my morning walk. It wasn't until a few years later that a friend asked me what I was doing. I informed her that I was being polite by saying good morning to people I passed. She reminded me that I would probably pass hundreds of people on a morning walk in Central Park so I may want to rethink my overly abundant friendly nature. She did have a good point, so I decided to limit my exuberance to those on my block and then shelve it until the next day.

How often do you walk up to a deli counter sharing little to no eye contact, maybe because you are texting or looking at emails, and order a pound of roast beef? Absent are the words of *hello* or *how are you* as your busy life has somehow disconnected you from being courteous and engaging with another human being. No wonder so many in the service industry are ticked off after two hours at work, and no wonder the deli guy slams the roast beef down on the counter as he calls out for the next number in line.

This week connect to others who you may interact with for only a split second or a couple of minutes. Offer a hello to strangers you pass when walking your dog, the mailman, the bus driver as you get on the bus, or the people with you on an elevator. You're not trying to get a new best friend on an elevator ride but merely working to connect to another. You'll be surprised as some people look at you as if you have just landed on the planet, while others will be completely taken off guard as they murmur hello. Don't take anything personally. I always giggle when someone guardedly says, "Oh, hello." Long pause. "Where are you from?" I say, "Colorado," and he or she replies, "Ohhh, I thought so." Then I say, "But I've lived in New York City since 1985," at which point the person's eyebrows shoot up to his or her hairline. It's really funny and is my way to play with other grown-ups who didn't know I wanted to play.

If you already share a greeting with those who are unfamiliar, then take this week to the next level by personalizing your greetings. As you visit the local branch of your bank, your pharmacist, or neighborhood bakery, take a few extra minutes to learn the name of the person who assists you. Introduce yourself and start greeting this person by name. This opening will allow others to realize you see their contributions as an important connection to your life. In return they will be more attentive to your needs and preferences as you now address each other personally.

This week is about being open to connections with people, however brief, which in turn is allowing you to connect deeper within yourself. Momentary connections allow your spirit the opening for opportunities of every type to flow in your direction.

Connect. See you next week.

MAY

Honor Your Energy
....

By now everything outside is in bloom and you are finding new parts of your life blooming as well. The energy you put out to the world provides the confidence needed to interact with a particular person or task. There is the other part of you which is disconnected from some of your power and therefore that energy is stagnant. As you continue working to honor your energy by connecting to others, the earth, and the good of the planet, you become further aligned with your vitality and exuberance. You will use this energy to propel your best intentions forward today and in the future.

Supporters will help push your boundaries, allowing you the opportunity to extend yourself and see things in a different light. But for those who do not hold your best intentions, draw the battle line to ensure protection. You will know when it is acceptable to alter your boundaries and reevaluate your limits as potential change will cause no feelings of shame or embarrassment. This is the true litmus test. This is the month to go into combat to reclaim your energy and continue to work on realigning and connecting to your truth.

First Sunday in May: Honor Your Line

This week decide where to draw your line in the sand on matters of importance. Back in the day my mom insisted that I have a clear understanding of my boundaries on issues of temptation before I left the house. "Know thyself and know thy boundaries" became her slogan for my teen years. Think about who creates pressure, by either asking or insisting you move your line, and why they're pressuring you. Be honest. If this person has your best intentions in mind, then this is not where to look. Examine what is negatively impacting your energy and work to remove those blocks, the very blocks that may be sabotaging and circumventing the positive energy that could be flowing into your life.

Could it be that you are pressured by a toxic relationship, have been asked to do things that are unethical, or encouraged to participate in an act that may cause legal problems? Maybe you have to examine where to draw your line in reference to cheating on a test and question if it is within the scope of your integrity. Sometimes it is easy to be influenced by those who tease and judge your ability to have fun with respect to the issues of alcohol and drug use. Understanding where to draw the line and the consequences of driving intoxicated need to be evaluated before you put the keys in the ignition. Quite possibly there isn't a *someone* asking you to continually compromise yourself, but the continued compromise is due to internal misguidance. This week examine how various choices interfere with your ability to draw and connect to your line.

During my teen years I wanted acceptance. At fourteen, I was invited to a slumber party hosted by the cool girls. I was elated. As the party progressed, with no adult supervision, ideas of toilet papering homes quickly accelerated to egging houses and cars. You don't need an IQ of 187 to realize that defacing other people's property can cause a lot of problems. I called my mom to pick me up and was immediately labeled as a spoilsport and a baby by the cool girls. While my feelings were hurt to once again not be considered cool, I also knew that I had no desire to experience restitution, so I headed home.

At this time I had a successful neighborhood babysitting business, which opened the door to meeting many wonderful families and cash for my future car. The next morning the father of one little boy I babysat was at our front door, and may I add he was an FBI agent. He inquired about the prior evening's destructive rampage through the neighborhood. Bingo—I sang like a canary as there was no way I was going to the big house! The girls had been spotted by several neighbors and this father wanted to know where they lived. They were all brought to justice (neighborhood style), as they had to scrub, paint, and clean up the messes they had made. At that point I realized I'd put the corners into my identity as a square and that was okay with me. Knowing where I drew my line in the sand and being considered a baby felt great.

Not every line drawn has to be life altering. Everyday issues can throw you off balance too. Take a small step. You may have the friend who makes you wait forty-five minutes every time you meet, yet you still wait. The inability to realize this individual is not honoring your time, but abusing it, probably makes you grow angry or feel badly about yourself. Draw your line and move forward. Wait ten minutes and then order your food or leave, as your time is valuable too. Do not fall into the trap of all the excuses, yours or your friend's. Realize that once you can put voice to where your boundaries are on the smaller issues, you will grow braver and become more connected to the bigger issues. Over time it will become easier to let someone know that you will not do something when it is disconnected and outside of your boundaries.

Take a day or two to contemplate where your line has been and where you'd like it to be. This is the week to get out the chalk and draw the line or follow in the footsteps of siblings by using masking tape to create a barrier and mark your territory. Either way, work on the connection to visualizing and establishing your boundaries.

Good luck with your move. See you next week.

Second Sunday in May: Honor Yin and Yang

This week you may discover your level of tolerance isn't exactly where you would like it. In fact it may not even be neutral. Conversations about religion, money, and politics, to name a few, can become heated, triggering actions that may surprise you and be considered irrational.

When I was a debater it was common practice to switch sides of the argument from debate to debate. This was a great tool for thinking quickly, using the power of persuasion, and tapping into seeing the opposing view. It's like the saying "You should walk a mile in his or her shoes." The key to tolerance is the capability to hear and see issues from a new perspective while building a connection to limitless understanding. In real life you probably don't sit around doing the debate exercise with friends, although it might be interesting.

Listening calmly to the polar opposite viewpoint allows for new information to be put through the filter as you see an issue from a new perspective and practice tolerance. Adjust to the principle that controversial issues in life cannot always be viewed as black or white but in varying shades of gray. You may be given concrete evidence and confirmation that you are on the right road while the opposite spectrum may allow for new ideas never imagined. Closing your mind makes for a very small world.

The decision not to tolerate a person, group, or behavior based on nothing more than the inability to examine a different viewpoint or philosophy can lead to discord. A bully gets the idea of intolerance from another and with cowardice follows the crowd. Choose to be a leader as you agree to explore and listen to the opinions of others and encourage sharing ideas and knowledge. There should be no coercion to control others but only to understand that tolerance is a key element that connects you to sit comfortably in your own power.

This week open yourself to seeing and hearing what the world and others have to offer. Try listening to a different political commentator. Catch yourself when you begin to judge and shut down without listening in full to the opposing idea before casting your vote. Read articles with varying viewpoints with the intention of broadening your knowledge for understanding both ends of the spectrum. You do not have to believe in any new concepts, change your religion, or join a new club. But when you offer understanding, patience, and tolerance to others, you offer these gifts to yourself as well.

Give a little yin; take a little yang. See you next week.

Third Sunday in May: Honor Mother Earth

There are many ways to connect with and honor the earth, as seen last month on Earth Day! Perhaps there is a spot on a windowsill where you can begin to nurture a plant. Maybe you can connect to the earth by planting a vegetable garden whose harvest will nourish your body. When I was a child, my mom was big on recycling. Unfortunately, at that time it was not very common. She was a pioneer in the area of recycling and not many other people shared her passion. She worked diligently to organize a community paper drive, loading thousands of newspapers, magazines, and phone books into the back of our pickup truck. She then drove to a centralized location where the volunteers were busy organizing and bundling to save the planet.

I was about six or seven years old and couldn't lift or carry too much at one time, so in her infinite wisdom Mom gave me a very special job. My help was needed after the bundles were wrapped with twine, at which time I was called to place my "magic" finger to the top of the bundle to create a perfect finish. It was my finger that applied the precise amount of pressure needed to hold the twine as the knot was made. To this day I take my recycling seriously as I remember the magic of my finger and the journey of my recycling efforts.

This week contemplate how you can make a difference and connect into honoring mother earth. If you are a litterbug, you already know what to do. If you do not separate plastic and metal, work to recycle electronics in your community, or compost, now is your chance. Maybe you would like to work actively with a local school by further defining this mission and educating the kids. When you pass by separate trash cans for newspapers, soda cans, and garbage, do you throw everything into one container and let someone else worry about saving the planet? Then this is your week to start noticing the varying trash cans and start disposing of your goods in a more environmentally friendly way.

Become cognizant of how you can make a difference. Think of one option that you can commit to and connect with that honors the earth. You may begin by cutting your use of paper towels in exchange for a sponge. If you already have a head start then maybe this is the week to embark on recycling your bags at a grocery store. Take the steps to implement these ideas into your daily, weekly, and monthly routine.

Everyone benefits and enjoys a cleaner, greener planet. See you next week.

Fourth Sunday in May: Honor What You Admire

This week you are going to look at the individuals who get your attention and the qualities you admire in them—those who make you wish you had more of that "special thing," whatever it may be.

For instance, there's the guy in the office who tells the truth about everything and it always works out in his favor. It would be great to be that honest, but telling the truth tends to blow up in your face, so it's easier to lie; I mean *stretch* the truth, wink. You also catch yourself admiring the woman with an extraordinary amount of integrity that others seem to respect. Maybe you look at a friend's tenacity and what he has been able to do in spite of his circumstances or contrary to what anyone said he could do. Wow, how nice it would be to have some of that. Well, you've come to the right page.

This is the week to decide what one quality you want to reconnect with. After all, you already have these qualities; you just need to tap into them. You only need to pick one attribute and decide how you will plant the first seed. If you're looking for more respect, then start saying what you mean and connecting to what you want. If you have told your children to be home by five o'clock and they continue to disrespect your request by arriving at five fifteen, it's time to advise them that there will be consequences if this behavior continues. Decide what that will be, share the plan, and if tested, move ahead with the course of action. You must follow through on your prior conversation. You cannot draw your line in the sand and then get a weak stomach when your line is tested. People who are respected mean what they say and say what they mean. Being firm does not mean you are angry, bitter, or volatile. It is merely a different way of communicating what you need and expect.

If your desire is to stop being untruthful and misrepresenting the facts, make the choice to go with honesty starting now. Life doesn't have to be a sugarcoated land of leprechauns and most of us don't expect that. Rainbows—yes, leprechauns—no. So often men and women are teased and chided about their dating and relationships, and this teasing can become uncomfortable. If a woman had a terrible date, she may choose to pretend it was great for fear of viewing this bad experience as a poor reflection of her. There is no need to pretend that you went to a five-star restaurant and got flowers. You don't need to say he is an amazing guy but you're not quite sure he is your type. Let me let you in on a secret: we all know you are fibbing. Who wouldn't want to see this imaginary guy again? I want to see him and I'm married! Once you can admit this was a humiliating experience because he was a dud or maybe you were stood up, you might be in for a surprise. Others will rally and share genuine empathy about something that was awkward and uneasy to share, but clearly not fatal. There may even be a silver lining that you never imagined as a friend may know a friend, a cousin, or brother looking for love. Maybe this is possible because you stepped out of your imaginary land where all of life is perfect and has lots and lots of leprechauns.

You may know immediately what you have been admiring in others yet not connected to within yourself. However, if you are unclear, take a day to connect to what you admire and establish how you will begin. Leave the leprechauns at home this week, but continue looking for your pot of gold.

When the rain stops, there are always rainbows. See you next week.

JUNE

It's Summertime; Go Out and Play!

· · · · · · · · · · · · · · · ·

When I was a kid, my family lived in a magical place: Medford, Oregon. My mother, as mentioned previously, is originally from Chicago. She often mentioned how Medford, in the late '60s, was smaller than the O'Hare Airport. While I had been in and out of O'Hare to visit my grandmother, this statement had no context or relevance to the magic fairyland that Medford was for me.

Medford represented fireflies, picking blackberries, Harry & David pears, camping trips, and fantastic wildlife. I was fascinated by and on a continual search for two things: tadpoles and caterpillars. We lived by a pear orchard that was bordered by a drainage ditch, and it was there I took my emptied Skippy jars. I'd search for the biggest and fattest tadpole swimming in the dirty water and scoop him up. He was mine. He would come home with me to stay in our garage, since my mother would not allow him in the house, and then I would wait for the magic to begin. I knew it wouldn't be long before he would transform into the most beautiful little itty-bitty frog. Once the transformation had taken place, I would take him down to the ditch and release him back into the water to his rightful home. And my search for more tadpoles would begin anew.

Even more fascinating for me were caterpillars; not all caterpillars, the beautiful striped ones that would make pale-green cocoons and then emerge as monarch butterflies. I had a keen set of eyes for those caterpillars and cocoons, and I could spot them fifteen to eighteen feet up in a tree. Once I saw what I wanted, I set out to get it. I would climb the tree never once thinking about how high I was going or how I would get down because I was after magic, the magic that these creatures would provide. And I could capture that magic because I carried my trusted Skippy jar. Understanding their metamorphoses were in my hands, with skills like a surgeon, I carefully removed the cocoon from the trunk of the tree using nothing more than two small twigs. Without hesitation my steady hands slowly placed the twigs into the properly prepared dwelling that I held immovable between my knees. The chrysalis had a new home, as prior to the procedure I had prepped the jar with a two-inch cushion of soft grass, extra twigs, and a perfectly perforated jar top to provide ample circulation and fresh air. Numerous twigs kept the cocoon propped up yet dangling toward emergence and freedom. If I fell out of the tree or dropped the jar, the cocoon would become unattached from the twigs and fall deep into the grass bed that I had prepared for the butterfly that was not yet ready and would now never emerge.

This was serious stuff and not to be taken lightly; therefore, I would wait for some help getting down from the tree. I trusted that some boy in the neighborhood or more than likely my brother would come to rescue me and my treasure. I never panicked. Instead I enjoyed the view from high up in the tree and spent time talking with my newly acquired friend. There I was, a towheaded child with pigtails, high up in a tree, casually leaning against a branch without a care in the world.

Years later, actually decades later, my mom and I were talking about my monarch butterfly years. She mentioned that I had been like a little lonely caterpillar who had spun a cocoon, reemerging from the chrysalis as a beautiful monarch butterfly. I then had flown away to find my way in the world. Where I would land was still to be determined, but when the decision was made, it would be beautiful. My mom assured me that I was no longer a caterpillar but instead a stunning butterfly, embracing all that life had to offer.

When we see something we want in our lives, we must give permission to our small, brave, adventure-loving child to connect and go after it. Give yourself the liberty to dream big without the fear of getting stuck. You must climb that tree of adventure without putting limitation in your way. You will be able to get down if this is not the right path, and you can figure out how to do this if you are equipped with no more than two little twigs and a Skippy jar. And if you get stranded, really stranded, stay connected, and trust in the universe. Trust the path as you calmly enjoy the view from the top of the tree and are in the moment, believing someone will show up to help you. How? Why? Because you have done your part, and when you have done your part, the universe steps in to do the rest. In my case it was my brother who would find me, rescuing my little jar of treasures that held the power to harness my dream, which was to become a beautiful butterfly transformed from some fat, awkward, little caterpillar.

First Sunday in June: Play like a Kid

Look back at a passion from your childhood that you have disconnected from and forgotten. It might be something you loved to do as a child that you were forced to give up or told you had outgrown. Growing up in Oregon and Colorado allowed for numerous camping trips for me, and you might be longing to repeat your days in the great outdoors too. You may not have a tent, camper, or mobile home, but is it possible to drive to the mountains for a hike or to spend one night in a cabin? Another option may be to sleep under the stars in your own backyard. If you loved baseball, then go to a game or a batting cage, and if bowling was your passion, it's time to visit a bowling alley and put on those goofy shoes—now there's a memory—and bowl a game or two.

You may no longer be physically able to climb trees, but you can sit under a tree watching the clouds roll by and daydream. Reconnect to what you lived for when the pace was slower and you didn't have much responsibility. Give yourself permission to partake in and connect to your childhood passion at least once this week, and try to do it twice. If you are really lucky and can do it for all seven days, go! Reconnect to playtime. Venture out on a limb and know that you are supported, as branches do not break away from firmly planted roots.

Go and reach up to the sky. See you next week.

Second Sunday in June: Play at Silly

We can all stand to loosen up a bit and reconnect to our silliness. From that place springs joy, and joy gives way to great happiness, which in turn takes us to the fountain of youth. Okay, now you're paying attention.

I am blessed to have two people in my life who are able to embrace silliness, Wayne and my mom. Nine years ago, Wayne started our tradition of elevator races and it is exactly as it sounds. We get on two separate elevators and race to our apartment where the victor is crowned! The crowd cheers, and the winner walks back and forth in the hallway while waving to the imaginary fans, signing autographs, and accepting the trophy. It's a good thing none of our neighbors have ever come out in the hallway to witness this, as they would surely think we are nuts. At times I think we are nuts, but it is so much fun to win. However, I didn't always embrace this silliness.

The first time this happened Wayne quickly ran out of the elevator we were both in, leaving me to hold the door open for about fifteen seconds before the doorman laughingly informed me that I had been ditched. I was confused and not too happy when the elevator I was in arrived upstairs, as Wayne was already there. I quickly asked Wayne what he was doing. I didn't realize he was being playful, but after that I was out to win. One of us still ditches the other to race upstairs for the win, victory walk, and crowning. This is playful and childlike and unleashes something inside that makes me giggle and my stomach flip-flop with joy.

One of our neighbors is three—well, actually our neighbors are adults, and their baby is three. From time to time he comes over to visit, and he can be pretty funny.

Usually when he leaves, he will say, "See you later, alligator" or "After a while, crocodile." Both of these phrases connect us back to the silly phrases of childhood. Can you remember the silly phrases from your childhood when you thought you were the smartest and coolest kid on the planet?

Find what makes you giggle with childish delight as you get lost in the connection to silliness and fun. Call someone and ask if their refrigerator is running, and if they reply yes, ask if it's running down the street! Watch an old cartoon, read the comics in the paper, or look at old yearbooks and the silly things your classmates wrote. This week explore and connect to childlike play as you spend the week laughing at all the stupid stuff that you are usually too mature to laugh at!

Supercalifragilisticexpialidocious. See you next week.

Third Sunday in June: Play at Nothing

This week enjoy connecting to nothing. Remember when you were a kid and your mom sent you outside to play? You had absolutely no idea what you were going to do, but you made it work. Sometimes you and friends would lie on the grass, looking at the clouds as if they were a giant Rorschach test, and debate whether one particular cloud looked like a giraffe or maybe an elephant with its trunk up in the air. You were doing nothing. But at the same time you were doing everything.

Have you ever watched a child outside? One minute they are heading in the direction of the swings, and en route they see a bee buzzing around some flowers and immediately become all consumed, forgetting where they were headed because they must explore what that bee is doing. Suddenly a big dog comes along and this now takes precedence because it is bigger and much more tangible and fascinating. Children do not focus on the future and therefore connect to the moment and what is happening now. Anything unplanned that comes their way is pure unexpected excitement and must be given some time and attention. Just like Seinfeld, it is nothing, and yet it is everything.

As Seinfeld's nothingness revolutionized television, this week let the art of nothingness revolutionize you. Constant overload is causing your attention span to become shorter. Start your week by giving yourself one hour to do nothing and if that allotment of time makes you scream, "What?" then commit to fifteen minutes a day. Allow that time to unfold to what you need, which you may not know at the beginning of your week. Sometimes when meeting a friend on the spur of the moment with no agenda other than to catch up and check in, you have the most revelatory conversations. See how many times during the week you can grab ten or fifteen minutes of nothingness to daydream or absorb into something that you would normally not give yourself permission to do. During this time set aside all lists, schedules, agendas, and phones.

Unfold into nothingness. See you next week.

Fourth Sunday in June: Play with Your Impulses

As a child you were probably taught to harness your impulses. As an adult you struggle to reverse those instructions while trying to reconnect to spontaneity, realizing this tool is needed for creativity. It's a bit of bait and switch being a grown-up and needing to access your impulses but realizing how deeply buried they are. What a mixed message. This week you get to play with your impulses, so bring it, and bring your A game to the party. Whether you run around a big city or hang out in a small town, make an effort to tap into the impulse game. Be open, and recognize when you have an opportunity to follow this path.

A few years back I was in Riverside Park during a snowstorm, and many kids had come out to play. Those who didn't have a sled sat on big black trash bags and rode them to the bottom of the hill. Watching the kids with a big smile on my face, listening to their screams of delight, I couldn't help but remember my own childhood memories in the snow. Two little boys approached me and gave me my own trash bag, which I could now ride to the bottom of the hill. I'm not sure who was screaming louder, me or the kids. It was fantastic!

Chicago has a wonderful fountain in Millennium Park, by the Bean, which allows children to wade in its water and sometimes get sprayed from the large fountains shooting water from their mouths. Every year we visit Chicago and end up at the Bean and this fountain. We usually sit on the side (with the other adults) sipping a cool drink and watching the kids play. The last time we were there I decided to kick off my shoes and take a walk in the water. The water and laughter triggered a strong sensory memory of my childhood days and running through sprinklers. When I was younger, private swimming pools and clubs were not as available as they are now. Running through sprinklers was a big deal and something I looked forward to every summer. I remember the smell of the waterlogged grass, the feel of warm concrete beneath my feet, and the joy of how my bathing suit felt on me. A woman looked at me in the fountain in Chicago and said, "You are really brave!" I asked her to join me, but she shook her head and said she would look silly. I later saw a child peeing in the water and wondered if that woman really thought she would look silly or if she knew what was happening in the fountain.

As adults we are often intimidated from participating in what we perceive to be a childish activity, even though it is what we desire. We think we need the excuse of having a child present in order to engage in the activity. Remember that you don't need a child to engage in play, as you have your own child waiting to play anytime you are willing to access it. Part of the reason Disneyland is so successful with adults is because when there you feel justified acting goofy and connecting to your inner child. After all, what else is there to do at Disneyland except be a kid? And no one can judge you since they are doing the same thing.

This week give yourself permission to connect on a deeper level to your playful nature through your senses of smell, touch, taste, sight, and sound on a spontaneous level. Do at least one impulsive activity that calls out to your spontaneity. Be spontaneous to the joy, to the impulse, and do something that you may think you are too old to be doing. Spontaneity is about a moment catching you off guard, about letting down the wall and going with the desire, and for this you cannot plan ahead.

Go have fun! Swing on a swing and feel the wind in your hair, go down a slide and feel the hot metal hit your thighs, or eat some cotton candy and feel the sugar as it sticks to the roof of your mouth and your fingers. Don't mind if anyone gives you a strange look; those people are too encumbered by being "adults" at the moment and would prefer not to share your happiness and connection to joy. Realize that you are never too cool or too mature to jump into the pool of fun.

Enfold yourself in the wonder of all things impulsive. See you next week!

JULY
Embrace Your Independence
....

In the spirit that our forefathers fought for the freedom and independence of our country, you need to fight for your independence as well. Commit to embrace protecting the underdog and standing up to bullies when no one else will. Vow autonomy to walk alone when it's the right path, and be brave enough to admit when it is time to walk with another. Find your strength, and learn the difference between being dominated or controlled by others versus being confident to ask for guidance and advice.

The balancing act of independence is tricky but not impossible. Influence may be needed from time to time; however, you independently make the final decisions to propel your life in a forward direction. You may belong to organizations with specific ideas, but you remain independent to your own conclusions. This month embark on your connection toward more freedom and independence in your life.

First Sunday in July: Independence from Poison

Eradicating poison from your life is necessary but something you probably don't think about. Many of us are holding on to relationships that are toxic and we haven't weighed in to clarify why. Take a step back and examine how poison affects you at another level. When you eat or drink something spoiled or toxic, you get sick, and your body quickly expels the poison. Your body will go to battle to eradicate the germ and once again live independently from sickness and pain.

Being around a person or a group of people who are poisonous and toxic can destroy your spirit, and those people need to be removed from your life immediately. Of course this isn't always 100 percent possible because immediately quitting your job due to a toxic boss or coworker is not always an option. The strategy would be to have only minimal, business-related contact. It is not in your best interest to have a drink with this person after work or to invite this person to your home. Acknowledge there is no positive value they can add to your life.

Poisonous people are dangerous as they divisively work to demean and undermine your goals by planting seeds that destroy creativity and, most of all, your spirit. They are void of light and have lost their connection to the heart, so they excel at destruction. Whether working to undermine an idea, a dream, or your connection to any wonderful experience, their motive is if they can't have it, neither should you. Poisonous people extinguish the light on your path as you work toward a connection to discovery and creativity. Regardless of where you are now or how bright your flame is burning, you cannot risk the flame becoming extinguished by those who have rooted down into poisonous marshes. Wish them well, and protect yourself from being in the alligator-filled swamp when a meadow of butterflies is well within your grasp.

Many years ago I served on a board of directors, and it was one wild ride. At first it seemed fun, meeting new people and giggling about a few of the long-standing members' kookiness and, at times, downright bonkers way of doing things. Then the landscape changed dramatically as projects spiraled out of control and nothing was handled with ease or honesty. The people at the top of the organization were revealed to be quite deceptive and manipulative. The contention they caused resulted in the joy of the mission evaporating.

Newer members had progressive ideas that could have expeditiously moved projects forward to a smoother ending. This was too threatening to the establishment, so the surreptitious game of poison began. The corrosive undermining toward anything or anyone credible was alarming, and the poison magnified. I reminded myself that we are the reflection of what we allow into our surroundings and thought of the old saying of "Show me your friends, and I will tell you who you are." I realized I could no longer embrace this organization. It was time to say "Adiós."

Many of us have poisonous people in our lives, and most of the time we allow them to exist. They lie dormant while we wait for the next cruel strike. Perhaps you continue to accept the expanse of the poison by listening to their quick comments that undermine the partner you have chosen or how you honor your spirituality. They look for any way they can let you know they are superior and your choices are mediocre at best. Expel them like you would a bad shrimp dinner.

Spend some time thinking about who may be your poisonous person or persons. If there is no friend, coworker, or family member who is poisonous, then you will have what is referred to in football as a bye week. Be honest and objective as this is one of the best gifts you can give yourself. Once you have established who represents poison for you, throw down the gauntlet, and get started. Going forward, don't go on any more movie or dinner dates with this person, and find someone else to accompany you on your evening walk. Perhaps help to start them on a new path by getting them a copy of this book and signing it anonymously!

If you feel brave enough to share why you are moving away from this person due to their inability to treat you kindly and with respect, then go for it. Communicate your issues to this person thoughtfully and without bitterness as you wish them well in future endeavors and exit. (Example: "When we spend time together, I don't feel that you honor my needs, so for me this relationship has run its course.") Cutting ties from constant ridicule and cruel, subversive behavior will give you a sense of ease and comfort. If you are unable to practice releasing this relationship with honest communication, then you will best be served by being continually unavailable. This person will get the message and most likely try to move on to the next innocent, but that is no longer you.

Independence from poisonous people may seem like an immense undertaking, but trust that you can do this. Understand you deserve to live poison-free. Acknowledge how far you have mobilized and connected into your independence by giving yourself full disclosure to what you are willing to embrace and work toward. The goal is to continue moving toward and staying in the light.

No need to pick your poison; there's an antidote. See you next week.

Second Sunday in July: Independently Forgiving

This week move the magnifying glass into dark recessed corners with thoughts toward forgiveness. It is true that forgiveness can be a long road, but you must start somewhere. The next seven days are an excellent beginning. The moment to release grudges and the pain of mistreatment is here. Continuing to live in your anger and using the mantra of "why me?" will not aid in the positive direction you are heading.

Many of us have been mistreated, some more than others, and your feelings are justified in the experiences that have brought significant pain and suffering to your life. We must stand united on the platform that shares in the interest to actively move forward from the injustices. Holding on to the pain and grudges have you temporarily stuck, so it's time to work on this part of your life. This is the time to recognize that your strength, tenacity, determination to overcome any obstacle, and the ability to rebound have given you the resources to master difficult and tumultuous times in your life. You are still standing; you are still here! Everything in the depository of your life is from the melting pot of all the experiences, and this you accept. Clinging to past scars serves no purpose in the momentum needed to reach your nectar.

As dandelions are tossed in the wind, those innocent, fluffy, little seedlings spread into more obtrusive dandelions. It is time to quiet the winds of punishment as you begin the road to forgiveness, further commuting clemency to yourself. Holding on to anger and grudges makes your spirit tired and your body weak. You fail to see a marked change because daily it is immeasurable; however, through time resentment takes its toll and stakes its claim. One day the reflection in the mirror will call into question whose face is staring at you. Choose the reflection that is recognizable, and look as you are on the inside—beautiful and crystal clear like a mountain stream. You deserve this freedom and are working toward this result.

This week raise your consciousness by continuing to lift the shroud and bring some light to the existing shadows. Navigate this week by nurturing your ability and the process to forgive one person you feel has wronged you. Make the choice that you are ready to begin moving through this part of your pain. This is a gift to yourself. Through forgiveness there is freedom, through freedom there is independence, and through independence there is joy.

When I was seventeen years old, I had a beautiful classic 1967 Mustang in mint condition. A girl at school loved my car and asked her parents to buy her one that was identical, right down to the same color of paint. Unfortunately, they were only able to find a 1969 Mustang and my car continued to get most of the attention. This upset her greatly, and in her jealousy she threw acid on my car, ruining the paint. Long after the insurance company had my car repainted, and other students saw the evil in this girl while she acted as if nothing had happened, I was still holding on to all my anger and resentment. I began to realize that the acid that had ruined the paint on my car was long gone but continued to corrosively eat away at me. I really had to work on this forgiveness thing, and I am not saying this is all angels and sparkle dust, but the angels will help if asked.

The request for this week is to choose one person or incident that needs the focus of your forgiveness. Continue to persist in the momentum toward freedom and independence as it takes on a whole new meaning. Congratulate yourself that you are here and will do everything to commit to this week. Give this routine a daily mantra, while brushing your teeth, driving the car, walking the dog, or completing any other task where you can indulge in your own thoughts. Repeat over and over how you forgive _____ for _____. You don't have to be enthusiastic or believe the words; just trust there is something magical to repetition.

Forgiveness gives you the keys to a new car and the permission to drive away peacefully. Leave your shackles that once tightly bound you to pain and suffering in the parking lot. Forgiveness opens the pathway to great freedom, and you know what happens when you follow the yellow brick road!

Yellow or not this is the road for the week. See you next week.

Third Sunday in July: Independent of What-Ifs

Many people play the what-if and do-over game, although it is not always in their best interest. They mix dreams of alternative outcomes from past experiences with the wishes to make them come true. Replaying how differently you would have that one conversation if you could do it again, getting a do-over for the relationship that ended badly, and promising to study if you could retake the test—these are all fairy tales that won't come true. You have played the what-if game from time to time, but the reality is at this point you cannot do anything to change the outcome of any event from your past.

The what-ifs of yesterday are irrelevant, but what-ifs of today can still be created. By focusing on the irretrievable what-if of yesterday it becomes easy to paralyze yourself from living in today and stepping into tomorrow. The what-if game is a wonderful tool to opening up possibilities in the future if you are willing to exit the past. You may not have gone to college at eighteen, but what if you go now? Release the trap of hearing the same story that didn't go your way. Stop thinking about how you didn't say what you wanted and instead think about how you may say what you need the next time. A conversation with you, testing out the variables, will aid to get it right! Explore the what-ifs that are standing in your way as you clearly begin to remove the obstacles that will allow you to make a different choice next time.

Almost everyone has a what-if and a desire to turn it around. While wishing to change the outcome, the stark reality is that you cannot. And in truth, these pitfalls, though often referred to as failures, are the stepping-stones needed along your path to greatness. Situations that have not worked according to plan are not failures, as you made a decision that taught you a valuable lesson. They are the obstacles that will shift your perspective or catapult you in the direction you need to travel. View these stones as gateways that readily open to the enthusiastic adventurer ready to move forward. Work to avoid the thoughts that cast and dwell in criticism, and instead allow yourself to view this as a place to stop, regain your footing, refocus, and continue in the direction of your independence. It is best to forget looking over your shoulder at what could or should have been and shift the focus to today.

I have a passion for the stock market and trading stocks. Three times in my life financial firms have asked me to join their team and move toward a career on Wall Street. For a myriad of reasons I never moved in that direction. At this point in my life I could spend every day looking over my shoulder wishing I'd moved in that direction. Maybe I would have earned great wealth and prestige. But I also could have crashed and burned. I will never know for sure. I do know it is wasted energy wondering if my life would be better or worse because in truth I believe my life is exactly where it is supposed to be at this minute.

The mission of this week is twofold. First, define a recurring what-if from yesterday so you can work on the release today. Understand there are always new opportunities in the future and, while not identical, they will allow for your new perspective and skills to be carried forth.

Next, adjust your focus. Recognize an old what-if, and explore your options. When faced with the frustration of a difficult relationship, you'll know how to put your theories into practice and make choices to change the plan of action this time. If circumstances have not allowed you to be a teacher but you love teaching children, become a Big Sister/Brother, teach a Sunday school class, or lead a Boy/Girl Scout troop. Examine how missing the deadline for your presentation will now put your focus on accountability, practicing and planning how much rehearsal time you need, and opening your connection to mentor others with their preparation. And having poisonous people in your past will let you see them coming a mile away, and this time you will have a strategic plan to handle them!

Unharness the what-if of yesterday, as it serves no purpose in your today and tomorrows. Instead, use authority and boldness to anchor yourself in creating and realizing the what-if dreams of today. Understand there is no time like the present; this is the week to begin percolating as you start playing the new what-if game. You cannot relive yesterday, but today is always within your grasp.

What if you continue forward in this journey? See you next week.

Fourth Sunday in July: Independently Flexible

If someone were to ask if you have a flexible mind-set, chances are you would answer yes, as everyone insists he or she is flexible. I often asked this question to employees who prided themselves on their flexibility yet bristled at the suggestion to stay late for a meeting or change a lunch break and got angry if a conference call needed to be pushed back, as their day was already set.

I really understood flexibility when working in an obstetrics office; babies are on their own schedule and enter the world when they are ready! Every staff member needed to be flexible to reschedule and accommodate patients and their already-overbooked schedules. Sticking to only one way of doing things without the mind-set of flexibility was a recipe for disaster.

How often does someone throw a monkey wrench into your plans, causing you to become frustrated, freaked out, or just ticked off? Is this because you cannot adjust if your day is catapulted in a different direction? You may find yourself reworking the same problems the way you have always done but not progressing as you would like. Often the river of life starts to transport you in one direction or at a different speed than anticipated, and slowly you resist and struggle, clinging to what works or what you think works, and pushing for what you believe is best. And if the current gets too strong, you may just get out of the water altogether.

This week look at your flexibility or lack thereof. Chances are you know someone who seems to breeze through life, as if nothing can throw them off course. Maybe that's because they have learned to go with the flow instead of fighting it.

There is a wide river between doing nothing and having done everything possible and then at some point just going with the flow and taking the ride. Gently guiding yourself toward more flexibility allows you to continue opening yourself up to unexpected surprises, new experiences, and trust in your own wisdom to know the difference.

A dinner date stuck in traffic cannot be controlled any more than an airplane breaking down at your gate. If trying to get on every other flight has failed, it may be time to go with the flow. Sometimes you have to give up control, realize the limitations, and wait for the glory of the unexpected. It could be a revelatory path to a hard-learned lesson or the serendipitous meeting of the right person to move your dreams forward. If you can't get on that plane, maybe you're getting the alone time that you have been unwilling to give yourself. Sometimes you have to take a deep breath and relax and realize there are some things you cannot control no matter how prepared, organized, and smart you are.

When things don't work out for children, they may have a momentary tantrum but are malleable enough to move on. Adults get stuck in the idea of riding the river one way, *their* way, and forget they don't always need to fight the rapids. A smooth ride can prove to be quite pleasant and allows for a different view. This week work on going with the flow by testing your tolerance for flexibility. When it looks as though something is going awry, don't sweat it. Do your best to salvage what you can, and then release and see if the current feels any different.

Try casting a different line and see what you reel in. See you next week.

AUGUST
Release the Obstacles
·······································

It is time to recognize the importance of releasing both literal and figurative obstacles. Neither works in unison to the connection of your true self. Making a conscious choice to discontinue using your treasures in order to save or protect them disconnects you from the wonderful feelings these items generate and the joy they can offer. For example, maybe all the gratification from having a particular pattern of china has morphed into only using the china for special occasions, to lessen the threat of breakage. The new memo is to use the good stuff and feel your connection, the connection that brought you to these items in the first place. You purchase things because they evoke a feeling within, but you then disconnect from these feelings by keeping items stored away.

On the flip side, it can be easy to fall into the trap of collecting and accumulating objects while forgetting to release what no longer serves any purpose in your life. Guilt clouds judgment, causing you to hold on to items that no longer fit your lifestyle. When items rest idly in your closet you are disconnected from what you admire. As you move into a state of catharsis by shedding old hurts and resentment, you remove the items that are no longer useful or serve a purpose in your life. This month work to move this pattern forward as you evaluate what you're holding on to both physically and spiritually, and decide if it is serving a purpose in your life today.

First Sunday in August: Release the Good Stuff!

Note to self: your whole life can be a celebration! There is a misconception that we must use certain objects exclusively for a special occasion. Children do not share those limitations and often gravitate to using the pretty stuff—translation: the good stuff. As a little girl I was no different and would insist on going out to play in either my school or church clothes. In my mind play clothes felt and looked ugly, and I wanted to be glamorous when I played house, rode my bike, or even climbed a tree. Clearly this was not practical, but most five-year-olds are not.

When I was very young, my mom would often describe how plants, trees, and people gave off vibrations. I tried to explain how ugly clothes were not in my vibration and ruined my ability to run fast and be my creative self. I still lost that battle. She would explain to me (as all parents do), that when I grew up and bought my own clothes, I could wear whatever I wanted, whenever I wanted. And so I do!

On one of her visits to New York, Mom walked into my bathroom and, to her horror, found me scrubbing out the bathtub in a beautiful royal-blue cashmere sweater. I'll never forget the look on her face; she nearly fainted. I did not care and refused to take the sweater off. Some months later she once again found me doing this activity in a fuchsia silk satin blouse, which suffered a catastrophe when some of the cleaning product splashed my way, landing front and center. In a fit of panic I called for her help, but alas, bleach cannot be rinsed away. The moral of the story is that bleach bleaches, so while the good stuff is great to wear, be sensible about it!

The silver, crystal, and china couples lament over for

months after choosing patterns carefully and adding to their registries often remain unused. What is the point of having a crystal candy dish that never once receives beautiful candies but merely rests high upon a shelf, tucked away? Some of my friends won't wear their grandmother's jewelry, lest it should get lost. So then I ask, why do you have such pretties only to lock them away? A plate or bowl may be bumped or dropped and wrecked, but that's okay, as you will have delighted in using and enjoying its beauty.

If there were a flood, fire, earthquake, or any other disaster, the real tragedy would be in never using the good things so you wouldn't break, scratch, stain, overuse, or lose them. How crushing to feel the loss of your beauties through some sort of natural disaster as opposed to through regular use. This is the week to take the sheet off the chair and the plastic off the sofa because you've already painted or moved that favorite picture, so it's time to take the next step! This is the week to begin shifting your attitude toward using the good stuff. Set the breakfast table with your best dishes, wear the dress you were saving for a holiday, or wear your grandmother's necklace. Luxuriate in your pretties. Otherwise, what is the point of having them? Wear the dress now because you may lose ten pounds and it won't fit anymore, or it may go out of style, and that connection will have evaporated.

Connect to the belief that your everyday life is valuable enough to use the treasures, and yes, these are some of the things you are grateful to have! There are a plethora of reasons to celebrate and feel joy in the ordinariness of each day. Appreciate that you can fill it by using your beautiful belongings. Your life is meant to be filled with beauty, so use your beautiful things. And if something breaks or gets ruined,

I say the same thing to you as I say to my mother, "I enjoyed using it. I felt great and I got my money's worth." Did wearing that article of clothing make you feel the self-confidence of a rock star? If the answer is yes, you got more out of it once than having it sit in your closet waiting a lifetime.

Enjoy filling your every day with beauty. See you next week.

Second Sunday in August: Release and Purge

This week may hit a hot button as you open up the Pandora's box of your inner hoarder. Now you might be saying this is not applicable to you because you are super organized. While you may not be a hoarder, it seems that almost everyone has one closet, a couple of drawers, or a corner in the garage that would be mortifying to reveal. Examine what you need in your life, which will allow moving past the point of congestion, and begin the journey to release. This week define and conquer what tangible things you are ready and willing to release.

There is great joy in purging items that no longer serve a purpose, and my personal love affair with releasing things has allowed me to change my surroundings and lifestyle often. When I was about eight and my mom and dad would go out for an evening, my brother and I would move all the living room furniture around, with the help of our babysitter, as we saw the new possibilities. I would also take it upon myself to help my mother reduce what I thought was clutter by gleefully tossing things into the trash. I had no idea why any one person would need twenty or thirty magazines all filled with recipes. Now that I cook I know the answer ... oops.

Cleaning out a closet of clothing that neither fits nor is in style can be cathartic. Glasses that are chipped should be discarded. Books that will never again be read can be purged and given to another. What about that dingy emergency underwear in the back corner of the drawer? Get rid of it. If you have an emergency in that underwear, doctors will swear the real emergency is in your panty drawer and not on the gurney!

Work on releasing a minimum of one item a day, as this will change the holding pattern. Think of the experience like circling an airport in an airplane. You cannot change the holding pattern until the fog gives way to the clearing, the gate is open, some large piece of equipment has moved, and everything is back on track. The flow of energy works the same within you. If you continue to hold on and force yourself to use what is no longer needed or enjoyed, you are holding up getting to the gate, making it impossible to see what is out there when you disembark.

Continue to connect to the flow of energy by trusting the process of release. Some items will need to go in the trash and others will be passed on to new owners. Know the items you are moving along give you the ability to share with others. This week you have a choice as to how you would like to go about this task. The first option is to choose one area to purge—a particular closet, dresser, pantry, or so on—and dispose of the items that no longer serve a purpose. The second option would be to get rid of one item a day from varying rooms as you rotate through your home. It doesn't matter if you never used it or wore it—no guilt. This part of the mission takes grit and guts to gain the glory! So go for it, and remember what holds you back congests your life! Plunge into the pool of release and believe that there is enough water and you will not hit your head.

Opt to do more than tread water. See you next week.

Third Sunday in August: Release the Suffering

Often there is one thing you complain about over and over to anyone who will listen. Could there be an overzealous commitment to suffering with the idea of paying your dues in order to be rewarded in the future? If you internally complain that your boss, partner, or job are stifling your creativity, become more proactive about the issue. Waiting for the creative fairy to come to your house while sitting and suffering in silence is not a good option. You can better open the creative channels by taking up a new hobby or skill that might excite you and get the embers of creativity ignited.

There is no need to pay some kind of penance by suffering. It is unclear how that myth has perpetuated through the centuries; however, it is clearly ridiculous. It is true that you have stumbled, fallen, and gotten up. But unending, interminable suffering needs to be taken off your radar and released.

When I was a little girl, on most Sundays my family would buy a box of fresh, hot donuts. I have never really liked donuts, so this was not a big deal for me. However, I do like the jelly or Bavarian cream on the inside. You probably get where I'm going with this. I suffered through a lot of donuts to get to the good stuff in the center. One day in the infinite wisdom of a six-year-old I realized that I could pull the donut apart and bite the good stuff out of the center, therein bypassing all that dough. When I was finished, I would carefully wrap the remainder of the donut in a napkin and throw it away.

It took my mom a while to realize that I was only eating the stuff in the center of my donut, which in her eyes was wasteful. I was issued the ultimatum of eating the whole donut or nothing at all. I chose nothing at all because it wasn't worth suffering through all that dough to get to the middle. I could have fought with her, insisting on eating the donut my way and making the whole experience miserable, but quite frankly I just didn't care about donuts. It can be human nature to cause an argument pertaining to something you really don't care about just so you can fight and then wear the crown of the person who suffers the most. Let's be honest: sometimes that is an awesome title to hold.

There have been numerous occasions when you have probably told yourself to pay your dues and suffer to arrive worthy for what you want. Realize you don't need to suffer if you choose to be decisive, connect to your truth, and opt out of drama. Now I hear what you could be asking: her life suffering has been about donuts? No, I have suffered far more than my donut escapades, but this is a metaphor. And by the way, éclairs are my truth. I may have lost the battle (not getting to eat donuts my way), but I won the war. I didn't have to eat donuts at all—and there was no need to fight about that!

Work to find the center of your truth, and eliminate unnecessary suffering by deciding how to use your energy to connect into your happiness. It is not mandatory to persevere through endless lunch hours with those who contribute to your unhappiness; you can always choose to eat alone. Nor is it in your best interest to retain a so-called friendship with a poisonous person if that person constantly criticizes you. And if you really hate tennis lessons, then stop taking them. Understand where you are blocked and transition into your éclair as you release the myth that surrounds suffering. This week explore one area of your life that needs to be pulled apart so you can connect to the yummy good stuff in the middle. It's perfectly acceptable to remove the dough and dispose of it.

Bathe in your Bavarian cream! See you next week.

Fourth Sunday in August: Release Your Booby Trap

In my early days in New York City I was surrounded by those who did not have to support themselves. Their circumstances allowed them to pick up the phone and have money wired for any bill that needed to be paid. This was not my reality so I missed out on a great deal of fun and camaraderie because I had to work. There were pros and cons to supporting myself and I was 100 percent connected to the cons.

My favorite mantra during those years was "It's not fair." I chanted it often and loudly. It was not fair that I had to support myself; it wasn't fair that I had to pay for my own schooling, and it certainly wasn't fair that my mom wasn't rich! Many who viewed this from the outside agreed that it was not fair. Aha, there were others who ascertained the same conclusion that I had been cheated! I knew it, and we were all in agreement, so now what?

This mantra did not allow me to connect to the essence of what I was trying to accomplish. It cemented my ideas that I would not get what I wanted because things were not fair for me. I had to acknowledge and accept that life may not be fair but also relinquish focusing on the unfairness of life, as that was holding me in chains. It was I who held the keys to my freedom. The daily ritual of painting all the ways in which my life was unfair was the biggest injustice of all. Removing this roadblock opened more highways and byways than I had ever expected.

It took a long time for me to realize the positive side of those early days in New York City and having to support myself. When things didn't work out as planned, I was more than flexible and could move on to the next idea and keep going. I became resilient and independent because there were no other options for me. I was also very responsible because I was accountable for my actions.

One friend who had been enjoying this enviable lifestyle suddenly lost his link to great luxury. His muscle of resilience had been weakened, and when life didn't go his way, he tried to flex but was unable to roll with the punches and tried to commit suicide. During his recovery he shared his feelings of how I was lucky to support myself because I was at the mercy of no one.

This week identify and work on removing one of your booby traps. Are you the type of person to ask for help, continue to do everything yourself, and then complain that no one listens or assists when you need something? If so, this is the week to stand down and hold yourself accountable and allow others to help after you have solicited their participation. Maybe you ask a question only to answer it yourself and then criticize that no one participates. This week is about enlightening yourself and then taking those tools and using them for your betterment. Discover one of your hidden mantras that if replaced would open a spring of insight and potential to new opportunities. You do not have to be perfect, nor do you need to hit a home run the first time up to bat, but you need to pick up the bat. By swinging, you will see the impediments start to dissipate, and the bigger obstacles will become easier to hit out of the park.

Get rid of the booby traps since they hurt too much when they go off. See you next week.

SEPTEMBER
Back to School, Back to the Basics!

·················

Most of you would agree that attending school has endowed you with many gifts; the most obvious is a broad base of knowledge and information. The September ritual of returning to school pulled you toward the continual stream of learning and broadening your horizons. You may be out of practice setting goals, but it's advantageous to get back in the game the same way you did in your early days. Of course time lines are met when it comes to a boss asking for something or picking up a child at practice as those deadlines are expected in your everyday life. What you may need is to connect to the ideas deep down that you rarely and maybe never have the time for.

This month link into and connect to your inner student. If you are currently in school, these exercises will help fine-tune what you need in the other subjects you are studying. Whether or not you liked school and whether you were a jock or a nerd doesn't matter. This has nothing to do with any of those long irrelevant issues of the past or present. This is a completely different trajectory.

When I graduated from college I was finally liberated from homework, free from endless hours of studying and learning things I may never actually use. The air was sweet. The first September after graduation my mom had the audacity to ask me how I was going to continue to focus on learning new things. I remember staring at her as if she was just short of looking like a woman in a Picasso painting. There was one problem: she was serious. It took some time for this to sink in (several years), but I realized she was right. She didn't care if I simply chose to study a map to learn new driving routes to get to the same place in Denver, which by the way is what I did. It was about challenging myself, setting a goal, and being engaged in new activities. It took me a while to catch on.

First Sunday in September: Back to Goal Setting 101

As an adult you have more than likely gotten away from setting personal goals. A parent asks goals of a child and management in some form or another usually require this from each member of their team. But in your personal life you may have stopped conceptualizing and then working toward a goal. What is it that you would like to accomplish? This is a question with the potential for a huge payoff, if only answered. It's so simple, yet you may find yourself making excuses or having difficulty articulating your desires.

At the age of thirteen I asked my mother if we could go on a safari. In those days traveling to Africa cost tens of thousands of dollars, making this a vacation for people with great means, and that was not my family. I asked my mom to take me to a travel agent so I could get the necessary brochures for my dream vacation. In her usual way of being a good sport she schlepped me downtown so I could gather my materials. I jumped in the car and immediately opened the brochure and saw the price of $17,000 excluding airfare. My first question was "How much do you think it will cost to fly round-trip to Africa?" I wanted to have all the information before I set my goals and the plan of action.

This week once again remove the rearview mirror and start looking forward—forward to what you can have and will have if you put some pen to paper and write down your goals. Write a minimum of one idea a day to move toward accomplishing your touchdown. You may get sacked or drop the ball, but sooner or later the ball always gets to the end zone. It has to—that's how the game works. If you would like a new job, this may require some additional course work or volunteering some of your time to familiarize yourself with that particular specialty. You could possibly ask five people to help you with their contacts. Imagine a friend asking for your advice to obtain this same goal. Think of the ideas you would offer. Sometimes you need to get out of the way in order to think outside the box. Take your own advice as you verbally commit to what you want and begin to see the possibilities of your touchdown. Write down and visualize the most immediate goal you would like to see come to fruition.

Begin inching your goal down the field toward the goalposts. See you next week.

Second Sunday in September: Back to Vocabulary

There has been an unconscious movement toward changing our speech by creating tenses that do not exist and using words with no meaning for reasons of which I am not particularly clear. What is clear is that "we the people" need to improve our vocabulary! Wikipedia and Google make it unconscionable and impossible not to understand the meaning of words and, better yet, to up the ante by learning new words. There isn't any excuse in today's world of technology for not mastering a great vocabulary.

During school years you are taught and tested on your knowledge of vocabulary. This is not a silly exercise, as it gives you the tools to understand what is being said in conversation and how to write an articulate piece of correspondence. Don't be fooled by the side of your brain expeditiously enumerating how this is going to be a ridiculous exercise and a colossal time drain. It will not. Maybe you're not allowing yourself to see the value in knowing ten-dollar words, or maybe you're questioning who uses those words. Lots of people do if you listen to CNN, Sunday Morning with Charles Osgood, or any political commentator. These programs have articulate hosts speaking to people with developed vocabularies and well-fed brains.

Consider how much money is poured into studies that tout staving off dementia or how to keep the brain active and involved as one's age increases. Adding to your pool of information and continuing to keep your brain active is an important part of maintaining a vital life. Life expectancy is increasing due to the rapidly improving field of health care and medicine, but you don't want the body if you don't have the brain to match.

Join a Scrabble group, pick up a crossword puzzle, or try a word search. The point this week is about connecting yourself to new words. Play like a kid and reward yourself for each new word learned! If games aren't your thing, then download an App or sign up on a website to receive a new vocabulary word each day. This is one new email you should be in favor of receiving! You can enjoy working to incorporate one new word a day into your daily conversations and correspondence. It's easy to do and lots of fun.

Expunge the conundrum from vocabulary. See you next week.

Third Sunday in September: Back to Prioritizing

As you notice how easily you get lost in the numerous lists you have going at any given point in time, it seems as though prioritizing has become a lost art. Sometimes what you need is to take a step back to analyze what may no longer be a priority and to grant yourself permission to rearrange or expunge a list completely.

Think about what it was like to organize your thoughts and priorities when you were in school. You knew what papers to write and in what order based on their due dates. If you wanted to join a team, you knew the deadline for registration. The first step is about scrutinizing all your projects and dividing them into primary, secondary, and tertiary lists. Take a look at what is realistic for the moment and requires the most urgency.

One of the most obvious priorities is to pay bills on time in order to avoid late fees and interest charges. Often the mail pile just keeps moving around the house until you are forced to get this task done. This needs to go on your primary list with a date to be completed. Decide how important it is for you to cull your bookshelf and determine a deadline to organize the photos from your last vacation. It may not be important to sell some antiques until next year, so that can be put on your tertiary list, and maybe you have never really wanted to learn how to play golf, so scratch that one off for good.

This week also requires a connection to being honest about what is important to you and your family. The reason to-do lists keep growing is the protest against acknowledging what is no longer a fit, and therefore you continue to shuffle the lists month after month, sometimes year after year. Some items are on your lists long past the point of expiration.

Give yourself the flexibility to realize that a certain project no longer fits within the goals you have for your private or professional life. Some things need to be taken off your lists permanently, not because you failed to do them but because they no longer apply to what you want or need in your life.

Acknowledge how your needs and desires have changed, and allow your lists to become more manageable and a truer reflection of your priorities. This doesn't immediately get you through the list any quicker. However, realizing why a particular item is on the list gives you the necessary focus to work on that project. And the result allows you to cross it off the list once and for all!

My personal attachment to lists has perpetuated my need to set up primary, secondary, and tertiary lists for things I need to do at home, opportunities for business, as well as social and entertainment lists. The number of categories needed for your lifestyle may be fewer or more; that is completely up to you.

Begin your week by culling and combining all the lists. Be realistic and honest as to what does and does not apply to your life and home. Next set up your primary, secondary, and tertiary lists with tentative dates for completing the list items. As you cross items off your primary list and move other to-dos from your tertiary to secondary list, immerse yourself in the understanding that lists are fluid. They change as your needs change, so own the flexibility to move items around and delete what is unrealistic or no longer a priority. You are not trying to drive yourself to do everything or prove that you are trying to be perfect. Work on your connection to prioritizing and organizing what will work best for your life.

Continue connecting to the pertinent weekly work. See you next week

Fourth Sunday in September: Back to Bravery

It's easy to forget how much courage and confidence is needed to start attending a new school or begin a class with all new faces while learning some strange subject. In hindsight you were quite brave to continue day after day, plodding through the muck and mire, while listening to your inner voice and sticking it out for the greater good of what was to come in the future. But you did it; you are truly brave.

This week reconnect to the bravery and self-confidence that aided you while outside your comfort zone, year after year, as you achieved great accomplishments. Maybe you've been focusing on joining a committee or taking up a new sport but just haven't been able to move forward. Inviting friends to your home sounds like fun, but you may be nervous about your cooking skills and wonder if others will like your style of entertaining. Open up to the challenge of facing your fears and entering into new territory that can be both exciting and scary. Connect to the awareness that something is outside of your comfort zone, question why, and begin the forward momentum to expand your horizons into uncharted terrain.

Push your limits to go watch a movie by yourself or eat a meal alone in a diner if these activities are outside of your comfort zone. Be the first to knock on a neighbor's door or invite a new employee to lunch. Practice being the first one to speak at the meeting as opposed to waiting for everyone else and hoping time runs out. If you have an uneasy feeling in the pit of your stomach as you think of doing some of these things, then this is your connection to bravery.

Give yourself two tasks for this week as you work to conquer what frightens or intimidates you. Maybe this isn't the week for planning; instead tap into spontaneity as you acknowledge that pit in your stomach and take action. As you approach the store with the high price tags that are intimidating, this is the week to walk in, browse, and enjoy eye-to-eye contact with the salesperson. Give yourself the gift of stepping across the imaginary line that will allow you to connect to your bravery.

No need for caution; there's no yellow tape here. See you next week.

OCTOBER
Harvest the Changes
....

As you reap the rewards of your harvest, you glide into the month of October. You have settled in and understood your abilities to connect more easily to yourself and others as you continue to farm the fertile soil. October puts you on the trajectory for the last quarter of the year, spotlighting the value of your hard work and commitment.

First Sunday in October: Harvest Abundance

Several decades ago the country was unified in the belief of scarcity. Collectively many stated there would never be a billionaire, and it seemed as if there were only a handful of millionaires. Many of us were taught and consistently given the information that not everyone could have great wealth. Fast-forward to today. We have blown the roof off of millionaires; there are now millions of them. In addition, there are over one thousand billionaires worldwide. The traditional workplace has changed, making it easier to start a business, and our country has always supported the ideas of entrepreneurialism. The point is that it's out there, whatever "it" is for you! Maybe visiting exotic places around the globe is your dream, or lots of cash could be your "it." Possibly your dream is a huge house with a swimming pool and tennis court. The road to great abundance is no longer strictly through the fortune of a family.

All of these "its" are valid and possible, so be careful not to fall into the trap of believing you can't do it alone, it's too late, you're too old, or you won't be able to find your next customer. The idea that only those with the right pedigree can be wealthy is a fallacy taught to us by those who did not understand. It is the type of thinking that does not understand the infinite abundance of the universe. Many parents and grandparents meant well but were misinformed. The road to financial success is happening to those with business ideas, innovation, creativity, and motivation. You may wonder how this could happen for some and not others. It is because their brain maps are different. The financially successful folks have not been programmed with the scarcity chip but instead have been programmed with abundance in the age of technology and sky's-the-limit thinking. It's time to remove the obstacles and see what possibilities of abundance await you.

Some years ago I was having this conversation with a housekeeper who desperately wanted and needed more business. She was a terrific housekeeper but was more connected to scarcity than to abundance. She was positive there was no way to grow her business in Manhattan with thousands of people living within a few blocks of one another. She was deeply wedded to her connection with scarcity. She did not have business cards and had not asked her clients to contact friends or give referrals. She donated time at her church on Sundays organizing the coffee hour, but she had never spoken to anyone about her skills as a housekeeper. I asked her to try four simple steps: (1) Print business cards. (2) Discuss growing her business and leave cards with every current client. (3) Ask her pastor to list her services in the monthly bulletin. (4) Visit her doctors, hairdresser, and dry cleaner, giving them business cards and asking them to refer their loyal and trustworthy clients.

Several months later this woman told me she had so much business she had to turn people away, referring them to her sister-in-law. Now you may be saying that's so basic, and it is. When the brain starts to short-circuit due to the black void of scarcity, basic and obvious ideas are passed over because there is nothing left for you. I too nearly fell down the rabbit hole while writing this book. I started to have the fear that no one would like or, for that matter, read my book. Then I realized I was looking down the well of scarcity instead of up into the sky of limitless possibilities. I had to stop and spend a week readjusting my thinking, thus reworking where I was short-circuiting. I realized my book would have an audience because my voice is unique and different from others.

Begin the week looking at your beliefs and thoughts on scarcity; get it all out in the open. Then start connecting to the world of abundance and examine what your options may be. If you would like to continue your education, examine loans and scholarships, fill out applications, and start working on the essays. Take the steps to start a business by narrowing down your specialty, searching for a mentor, and beginning to work and write your business plan. Leave no stone unturned, and if your path is filled with boulders ask for some help in rolling them aside. Have fun clearing your path to abundance.

Climb out of the well, as there are no wishes at the bottom. See you next week.

Second Sunday in October: Harvest Change

While you enjoy spending time with friends there may be one or two people you would enjoy more if they thought or acted like you. You might have chosen a partner with the intent of getting him or her to change so all your dreams can come true. While you can ask another to listen as you express your desires for their change, gauging the extent to which that person is open to change, you cannot force another's hand. It is a waste of energy to try to maneuver another human being into and toward change. The real success is working on you. The only control worth having is self-control. This translates into the ability to change you and only you.

The real work in changing yourself is by mirroring the true reflection of who you are through connecting to what you wish to harvest. Tempering what you ask of another (on their course to modification) is tricky and often the shadow of what you wish to change in yourself. If you expect the winds of change to permeate your being, a willing participant must show up at the party: you.

Becoming annoyed by the behavior of another is often the catalyst for what you need to change. It is easy to disregard these feelings as nothing more than a list of what bothers you about others or the validation of having a bad day. Most often you know this is not the case. There is a clear line between sharing your needs and demanding that someone stop biting their fingernails, cracking their gum, or chewing with their mouth open.

This week pick one behavior or habit you will work toward changing. It would be rare to have only one thing in your war chest, but start with just one. Do not feel you have to jump in by choosing your Mount Everest, although if you insist, kudos to you. Change is made gradually, which allows the mind to start reprogramming for other avenues of your journey. Maybe you would like to stop your road rage, checking your phone every ten minutes, or another habit you're not proud of and are bothered by in others. Becoming aware and connecting to the desire for change is half the battle.

Examine the change you would like to make and take action. (1) Stop criticizing this behavior in others. (2) Stop making excuses. (3) Commit to changing this behavior and start practicing. You cannot stop texting while you drive if your phone is in your lap. Shut it off, or place the device in the backseat, out of reach.

Spend today thinking about what you would most like to change during the next seven days. Start with the connection to these seven days and see how much longer you can make this happen. If too much time is left for contemplation, you may find it is easy to avoid this week. Instead allow yourself to connect into this new goal that begins slowly but may turn into fourteen days, then twenty-one, and so on. Change is gradual and at times feels tedious and insurmountable, but Mount Everest looks so much better from the top.

Work to change the view. See you next week.

Third Sunday in October: Harvest Many ...

In third grade I remember my teacher asking us about our favorite colors. When it was my turn to answer, I proudly responded that I had not one but two favorite colors, to which the teacher replied I could not. I looked her right in the eye and said, "Yes, I can because my mom said I could." She had no idea whom she was dealing with. Not only was my mom the rule maker at my house but probably for the whole universe too, so that teacher better watch it.

I am always amazed by the concept of favorites. Why do you limit yourself to only one? There is no written rule that states you must have only one favorite of something. I have two favorite colors, always have and always will, and my mom said it is okay! If I knew my last meal was coming I would have Peking duck, salmon, and crab legs drenched in butter, fettuccine alfredo, and New Zealand ice wine. Then I would have not one but two desserts: crème brûlée and a lemon tart. This had better be my last meal; otherwise a combination like this will surely kill me! The point is these are all my favorites, so why must I be asked to pick only one?

There may be times you wear a favorite shirt or a favorite pair of jeans over and over. Your mind-set has narrowed, never contemplating wearing something else because you are stuck in the mode of a "favorite." Even Oprah's list has twenty-five to fifty favorite things, every single year. She understands the value of not limiting yourself to one favorite thing! Very often it may be comforting to go back to the same old familiar favorite when instead you should think about venturing out to taste, explore, or read something new.

Adults often ask children to pick a favorite food, teacher,

or toy. This creates the notion of consistently choosing one particular item over all others. Since children don't see any limitations, a little girl may tell you that she wants to be a nurse and a teacher, while a little boy may say that he wants to be a fireman and a policeman. They are fluid with the moment and cannot comprehend limitation which is really the premise behind having a favorite.

On the flip side, adults are often locked into the idea of limitation, thereby laying the groundwork for potential missed opportunities. (Remember, in June, playing with your impulses will lead to all sorts of new adventures.) Sticking to what you think is the favored method to tackling an obstacle may be the idea that keeps what you want out of your reach. Limiting yourself is a learned behavior, so work on openness as you continue to explore and loosen up from always using the same approach.

Get out of your comfort zone by letting go of the tried and true favorites as you listen to a new kind of music or try a new type of food. Broaden your horizons and plan an unfamiliar weekend adventure, choose to read a foreign newspaper, take diverse routes to work, or try the other flavor of ice cream as your favorite steps aside. Start your meetings with a joke or a personal story, or allow others to share what they did over the weekend. Practice liberating yourself from the limitation of choosing only one way to live your journey. If the new experiences don't feel like a fit, you can always go back to your favorites.

This week shake things up a bit by getting out of the familiar swimming pool and head to the ocean. Continue swimming, but allow yourself to be introduced to larger waters. While the waves may present a bit of an obstacle, obstacles are only as big as you perceive and give them the power to be. Experiencing the vastness of possibilities the ocean has to offer while viewing the endless horizon may allow your decision to keep coming back for more!

The ocean is big but liberating. See you next week.

Fourth Sunday in October: Harvest Discipline

Think back to the studies that were done in reference to children watching violent television shows and how they were more prone to acting in an aggressive manner. Now think about all the commercials you see in one evening of television. Case in point, you head to the kitchen or think you need these products the next time you're at the grocery store. The subconscious mind is saturated with what is continually bombarding you all day and every day.

As the witching hour of 9:00 p.m. would arrive, I'd find myself with a sudden desire to eat ice cream. Then Wayne and I would make a quick run to the store so we could have a treat. We weren't hungry and didn't have a craving, but once I saw how fantastic the ice cream looked on TV, I had to have it right away! By the way, we would often purchase an extra two or three pints of ice cream for reserve so we could save ourselves the trip to the store in the future, or that was the logic. This might be a good time to have only one favorite and not choose many!

We realized we were eating ice cream five out of every seven nights of the week, and that isn't a good option for a late-night snack week after week and month after month. At first I made the excuse that this was a great way for me to stave off osteoporosis and get my daily dosage of calcium. Wayne's retort was handing me my bottle of calcium supplements and wondering how I was suddenly unaware what these were for. He promised to do a better job in the future to help me. Talk about a killjoy! There he was just taking away the glitter. I could literally see it disappearing into thin air.

We made a pact that during the workweek we would not

leave our building unless it was burning down and would not go to the store after eight o'clock. We also agreed to eat ice cream only once a week. At that point I realized that I was about as disciplined as a puppy peeing all over the house. I had to take some time to think about how this was contributing to my sluggish mornings and the other effects on my body.

It is hard to be objective when looking at where you need to instill a bit more discipline into your daily rituals. You may need to rethink how many times you hit the snooze button before getting out of bed in the morning or question if you plan enough time for your response emails if they have typos and do not contain the content you had hoped. Perhaps you need to stop eating anything after nine o'clock, or maybe you need to go to bed a half hour earlier. If you don't have enough time to learn something new, cut down on the amount of television you watch to one hour an evening.

This week implement more discipline into your life. Choose one thing and hold your focus in that area for the week. Do not trick yourself by making a hasty decision that this week does not apply to you. Instead take a day to decide how to embrace this week and then put the playbook into action. Do you need thirty minutes a night to finish a project or reintroduce that extra time for evening walks? Possibly you'll choose to be accountable to the discipline needed to carve out some time to stay tapped into playing like a kid and being impulsive.

While this is a challenging bridge to cross, it's sturdy. See you next week.

November
Thankful for Your Treasures
···

For those in the United States this is the month we celebrate the holiday of Thanksgiving. You may spend weeks in preparation for that one day while the resounding question of what you are thankful for swirls in your mind. Work on connecting to these thoughts while carefully contemplating the gifts in your life for which you are thankful. This month you begin to give thanks for your lessons learned and the awareness of the road traveled thus far!

First Sunday in November: Thankful for the Holidays

Here you are after the harvest, before the celebration; now what? It's time to revisit the list you made in January noting your ideal holiday season. Take the envelope out of the drawer, open it, and look at your wish list. If you didn't make a list in January, no need to fret; for instructions, refer to "Third Sunday in January: Reflect on the Holidays," and make your list now.

Like it or not, this time comes once a year, every year, and wouldn't it be inviting if you could make it stress- and worry-free, subtract the guilt, and reduce the debt. That's your goal! Think how you have imagined or agreed you would rework this time of year—the holiday season. Put into practice what you put on that list. Apply your tools.

This week will be split into two distinct parts: the side of you that wants to look at doing more and the side of you that would like to do less and not feel guilty. If your thoughts, desires, and wishes have changed from your January examination, that is okay. Recognize your desires are ever-changing and you are connected to the fluidity and movement, which means you are in tune to having the life you want.

Look over your list and ask yourself what you need your experience for the holidays to be. Connect into what will resonate as enjoyment this holiday season. Do more of what you love and less of the activities that cause you to feel stress. Allow yourself to soar and embrace the joy of the season as opposed to suffering from emotional and financial mayhem. Remember, your boundaries need to be crystal clear. When you examine what areas of your holiday season need a little adjusting, you will be able to define the changes that are important.

Consider where you want to focus your energy and consciously choose at least three of the items on your list that will bring you closer to a stress-free, happier, and easier holiday season. Start to actively concentrate and begin to share your strategic holiday concepts with family and friends. This is the year you ask for encouragement and support as you attempt to do something new and different from the past.

Begin relaxing into your season of celebration. See you next week.

Second Sunday in November: Thankful for Silence

In the same way any electronic device loses energy and has to be recharged, you need to recharge as well. When electronics are out of power, they stop working until plugged in and charged. But you keep pushing yourself and resist submitting to less power-down time. How often do you walk in your front door and instantly turn on the television or some type of music? You may immediately engage in a conversation on speakerphone while simultaneously doing some chores. While driving your car, you might chat on the phone, dangerously text, or change CDs. It seems as though enjoying or allowing yourself to be swept away by the pleasures from listening to and bathing in silence have all but disappeared. While you may not be a proponent of living in silence for months, allowing silence a small opportunity will be a great reward.

It is easy to automatically turn on the radio or television in the morning, and the evening news may play in the background as you eat dinner or some other program while you try to read the newspaper or a book. It seems the murmur of noise is always in the environment of life. The constant backdrop of noise may help to keep the focus on the task at hand; however, some quiet time can take you on a journey deep down into the well of inspiration. Fill your bucket with the creative juices and inspiration to break out and do something different. Many ideas are brought forth from the small moments of silence pondering the "what now?" and "what next?" questions, and when strung together fit as magically as pearls on a string. Silence, pure silence, can be golden. Sometimes the most brilliant revelations are born out of silence. Take some quiet time to be alone with your thoughts. In these moments let your dreams soar while you percolate on new ideas which can ripple in the waters of solitude.

Late at night your home fills with silence as the day comes to a close. Shutting off the television, computer, and your phone allows for that moment of *ah* as you relax into the solitude. That moment at the end of the day when you might hear the crickets chirping often feels like a breath of fresh air. Imagine if you could have more of that during your waking, conscious, creative day. Be aware of the power gained in the silence as you connect to your breath and the ideas that haven't found the freedom to escape because they were bogged down and trapped in the constant noise.

Allow for time in your day to feel the calm breath of silence during as many intervals as possible. Resist the urge to have familiar background noise turned on during the day. Concede time to discover and be with your own thoughts as you endow yourself to intermittent splurges of silence that will feed your soul. Start by breathing deeply and feeling the rhythm of your breath. Allow your breath to give you focus, as your gut will give clarity to the possibilities and what you can conquer.

This week work on a deeper connection to the virtue of silence. Avoid the impulse to turn on and plug in when you first awake. Instead take a few minutes to be in silence while you connect to the day. Connecting to the silence will unearth your buried treasure and direct you to your next discovery.

Shhh. See you next week.

Third Sunday in November: Thankfully Limitless

The year 2010 was one of great highs and a terrible low. February of that year my mom and I spent three and a half weeks traveling to India and Nepal. She climbed hundreds of temple steps and got up early to enjoy sunrises. No one could believe she was eighty-five. Later that year on a blustery December evening, while walking arm in arm, we tripped over a curb (that was only a few inches high) and fell. I knew immediately it wasn't good. She had fractured her femur and the Pandora's box of the road to recovery had just been opened. Surgery, bronchitis, flu, pneumonia, physical therapy, fractured vertebrae, more physical therapy, more fractured vertebrae; it was a long, scary downward spiral.

Late summer of 2011 my mom was back on her feet, literally, and informed Wayne and me that she was ready to get physically active again as she had missed that part of her life. With great enthusiasm she announced that she would be going back to tap class, as in tap dancing. To the best of my recollection, she was last in tap class in 1977. I know; we thought so too: there's only one word for it and that's crazy. But how could we prove it, as she hadn't fallen on her head, only her hip? She was excited as she told us how she would be exercising her brain learning new routines while also engaging new parts of her body. I calmly stated, "You will be engaging new parts of your rear because you will be on that more than your feet." It took a couple of months for her to let go and get past her desires for the long-lost hobby, and then she was off to the races again. This time she decided she wanted to go back to golfing. During that conversation I had to inform her that a cane could not, nor has it ever, doubled as a nine iron.

This is clearly a case of my mom once again seeing the glass half full—and also being highly delusional, but I'll leave that out for now. All kidding aside, this is someone who really stares limitation in the face and does not give in without a good argument.

This week think about where you may be placing limitations on yourself. If you were told in the second grade that you had two left feet but would love to dance, it is time to take a class. Tap anyone? And suffering from pitch problems can be corrected if you would really like to sing. Don't allow yourself to be disconnected by the limitations that are self-imposed or given by others. Give yourself permission to remove some limitations with just a little work.

You know the saying: the sky is the limit. See you next week.

Fourth Sunday in November: Thankful for 50 Percent

As seen in the prior week my mom is a person who always sees the glass half full, which at times can be quite annoying. Once when we got a flat tire on the highway, her first words were "Aren't we lucky this didn't happen late at night?" I responded, "Wouldn't we be luckier if this hadn't happened at all?" Living in Colorado presented many snowy mornings when she would joyfully enter my bedroom singing some crazy song and raving about the beautiful white blanket covering the lawn, trees, and cars. She was so happy at how beautiful the world looked; however, the tape in my brain thought, *What a sloppy mess*. I did not share her joy. As I got older, I realized she is right to view varying situations with an attitude of positivity and possibility. She has a direct link into the gratitude of anything that comes her way.

As I shifted my attitude toward finding the silver lining, certain limitations seemed to dissipate. A different perspective allowed me to view options and problem solving with sharper focus. Sometimes the mind-set of seeing the glass half empty causes the answers to appear continually blurry. Viewing the world through this perspective shuts down the ability to see possibility. Focusing on the negative and what comes from the negative, doesn't link you into the type of connection that is useful for problem solving and creativity.

This week if the winds quickly change direction, take a moment to see the glass half full and look for the possibilities you may have otherwise overlooked. If a day with outdoor activities is postponed due to rain, see the line in the water glass as you realize there is an opportunity to visit a museum or try a foreign film. If the meeting you prepared for is postponed, you could view this outcome with two different points of view: the first would be to think of how much time you wasted this week while preparing, time that could have been used to do something else. Or you could shift the focus by realizing you will now be prepared for the next meeting and don't have to do any work to meet this goal in your current week. The outcome remains the same, but the mind-set is completely different. Shifting the focus to what is working, successful, and positive will allow you to keep your balance in current situations and further open you up to seeing solutions. Viewing the glass half full lets you circle back to your connection with gratitude and all things wonderful.

Keep checking the water line; you can make it rise. See you next week.

DECEMBER
Time for Celebration
....

Here you are entering the twelfth month of the calendar, which in many cultures is a time of celebration. December can either unveil itself as a time of magic or mayhem. While you anticipate what is ahead, you can feel exhaustion or exhilaration. You deserve to celebrate while consciously choosing not to fall off a cliff.

December can be a wonderful month full of parties and dressing up in all sorts of fun clothes while enjoying tons of decadent food. You may veer a little off track and forget to nourish yourself with enough fresh fruit, vegetables, and protein, but that is easy to correct. Also the speeding train of credit card debt moves swiftly this time of year, so opt not to be a passenger. It always amazes and saddens me to hear the stories of those who have just paid off last year's holiday shopping spree only to start the cycle again. There is nothing celebratory in this type of out-of-control behavior. Someone who has a net worth of one million dollars does not spend two million dollars for the holidays, which is why they are worth a million dollars. It is within your power to change, and that is definitely something to celebrate.

Enjoying this wonderful season is perfectly fine, but stay in control, and practice discipline with regard to the choices you make. Three cookies can be just as satisfying as a dozen (see "Fourth Sunday in October: Harvest Discipline"), and one new dress can be just as beautiful as five. Abstaining from the thought process that everything is about quantity will aid you in staying on track. Don't get duped into believing the hype by those who wish to sell you more. Buying a bigger house will never give you a better life; it will only change your lifestyle, and these two things are not synonymous.

Do not convince yourself that more stuff equals greater happiness, as that is simply not true. The quality of your life will remain the same whether you spend very little this season or end up with a mountain of debt. If disconnected from your financial truth, you may be setting yourself up to take a bruising. So take a look at "Second Sunday in April: Connect to Responsibility," and relive your success in accountability. Learn to distinguish what is best for you without taking guidance from the outside marketing sources telling you to buy more. Strive to have a holiday season that is about quality time with friends and family where you can relax by being yourself, present in the moment, and disconnected from stress.

It's easy to fall into the mind-set of needing more than you use and using more than you should. But is this really what you want for yourself? Because it is possible to celebrate with moderation in mind. Don't get stuck with thousands of dollars due on a credit card bill, because that is a wicked hangover if you can't pay it off.

This is the month to celebrate embracing your truth and understanding what makes you great!

First Sunday in December: Celebrate Your Finances

Years ago I decided to opt out of office grab bags because I didn't need or want another CD of holiday music to add to my collection, another crazy pair of earrings that looked as if a seven-year-old had made them in an arts and crafts class, or another coffee mug. This kind of stuff was useless to me. I found out it was useless to everyone else as well. Maybe you work in the one office in the world enjoying this tradition, but my research has gone far and wide, and I haven't found it. Here are two powerful words: *opt out.* This isn't a requirement of any job, social group, or friendship. Once I opted out at several offices, it was amazing how many other people followed and were happy not to have the pressure of this particular activity.

Examine the ways you are pressured to spend money during this month all in the name of celebrating something. Instead work on your inner celebration, which will acknowledge not being broke or scrambling to pay your bills once January arrives. Your financial life will transition smoothly into the next year because you have been enlightened and able to quell the whispers to spend, spend, and spend. You will feel an empowering sense of accomplishment as you open an affordable credit card bill as opposed to wondering if you have suffered identity theft or spent the last thirty-one days held hostage by a persnickety pack of elves who have abused your credit.

This is not to suggest that by opting out of crazy grab bags you will find financial freedom; that's not realistic. Buying crazy ties your dad doesn't need, an itchy sweater your sister will never wear, or another household appliance your mom will never use are all ways in which your money may be wasted. Instead, consider the possibility of you and your siblings pooling your money and taking your parents out for a nice dinner. If you have a great group of friends but find overspending on annual gifts is a problem, it might be an option to agree to recycle gifts. Each of you can wrap and give an item you've received or never used and couldn't give away without feeling guilty prior to this exchange. Maybe you already released these items in August (see "Second Sunday in August: Release and Purge"), but if not, here's your second chance. If that doesn't seem feasible, why not make each friend a beautiful card, place it in a box, and have a brunch at your home? It doesn't have to be fancy, although you should always use the good stuff (see "First Sunday in August: Release the Good Stuff!")!

This is about thinking outside the box. You can objectively decide what is and is not within your budget and then stay the course. As the week begins, think about and write down five ways to rein in the spending during this somewhat-frivolous and fun time of year. It's not all or nothing, panties or commando; it's about further connecting yourself to the alignment of your needs. Have a great week increasing your financial bottom line, and keep in mind that money holds the vibration of freedom. Choose how much or how little freedom you would like.

Think of this comparison, as if watering a garden. You can use a sprinkler system, a hose, or a watering can, as all serve the purpose of getting water to the garden. One way is more time consuming and exhausting, while another way is speedier and involves less of your time, thus allowing more time for other things. It's a matter of personal choice; there is no right or wrong answer. You can continue with your little watering can, but it might be nice to eventually have a sprinkler system. For me that is equivalent to a savings account, real estate, and credit cards with a zero balance. Start to work on maintaining or putting money toward your sprinkler system.

Keep your wallet closed. See you next week.

Second Sunday in December: Celebrate Positivity

This week embrace sailing in the breeze of positivity, and view how reflecting this within yourself as well as sharing it with others, gives everyone a lift. Wayne has often said, "It's just as easy to find the good in people as it is the bad." When you think about it, that's a good point and reflects how we view things in general.

How often do you fill out seminar, vacation, or hotel surveys to criticize all the aspects that did not live up to your expectations? Think of all the hours spent waiting to speak with managers to belittle some tiny part of the experience that may have gone awry or some unsuspecting employee who wasn't perfect. Clearly this isn't about the rude employee who acted disrespectfully to you or your family or the resort that has done a bait and switch. Those situations call for constructive criticism and can be used as teaching tools for all involved.

While it is important to inform companies of how their services did not live up to expectations, it is just as important to take the time to share experiences that were fulfilled wildly off the charts. During check-in at a hotel in Germany, the staff commented that I would be with them for my birthday, which was in two days. I thought it was lovely they had noticed that information in my passport and shared early birthday wishes. On the actual day of my birthday the front desk employees and doormen all wished me a happy birthday. Upon checkout I made it a point to find the manager and compliment him on his staff and their hospitality.

This week take time to work on praising those who have made a difference in welcoming you to their cities, restaurants, and bookstores. Registering complaints has become all too easy; now work on taking three to five minutes to sing another's praises. As your positive comments contribute in building another's business or team, spirits soar in response to your appreciation for their hard work. Positive feedback also informs them what was important and what you would like to enjoy more often in the future. Focusing on the positive will allow you to feel more joy and link deeper into your gratitude.

Sail toward giving out the positive. If this is a new experience, take a day or two to find your sea legs and then proceed, giving you a remaining five to six days to sail. Share a minimum of one positive compliment daily with a person or organization that has met your needs and expectations. Thank others for their patience in answering all your questions, working with you to maintain your health, filling out the form for you, providing the extra towels, having exceptional knowledge of the team, or any other act of kindness. When you look to share in the good, the best, and the positive, it's like the world is in Technicolor and comes back to you tenfold!

Leave the black-and-white perspectives behind and enjoy the color. See you next week.

Third Sunday in December: Celebrate Your Weird

This week celebrate your weird! It is a cause for celebration when you can embrace marching to your own drummer and all the stuff that makes you different. Having come down a long road, you are ready to open up the kimono, so to speak, as you are at the intersection of embracing your afro, short pants, colored socks, glasses, and anything else that is the real you!

I know several people who will not wear their eyeglasses out of their homes as they do not want to be seen in public wearing glasses. Considering how stylish eyeglasses have become and how some celebrities wear them despite perfect vision, it's odd some are still embracing the weird-kid-with-four-eyes idea. It could be the same for folks who feel embarrassed they don't have the typical body, whatever that means. If you are not familiar with Lena Dunham, take a moment to Google her. This young woman has become the cover girl for embracing what is beautiful about being different and quirky. As a collective we have bought into the homogenization of our culture through the messages of the media and advertisers, so as individuals we have worked hard to look like everyone else. Connect to your quirks. It is what makes you marvelous.

It's true that copying someone is a form of flattery, but it's not really you until connected at the base of your truth. At the base of your truth lies the spark that will ignite the ability to connect. Let go of the competition, and stop trying to imitate or be someone else. Phrases and words that a friend or coworker spouts can make everyone laugh (seeming so incredibly hip) but sound awkward coming out of your mouth because this is not your truth but belongs to another. I remember in the '90s so many people pretended to like sushi because it was so hip, and wasn't that the goal, to be hip? That's a rhetorical question, as hip is not the goal—truth is. Hip happens when aligned to your truth, which is the real you. Diane Keaton can wear men's jackets, trousers, and ties all while looking hip and chic because she arrives in life present, from her truth. The truth allows her to align and embrace what her quirkiness is and that makes her hip and ever so cool.

How often have you been told to march to your own drummer only to find out that you are doing exactly what everyone else is or what you believe is expected, taking you further off course? My mom has always been able to follow her own rhythm, even when it wasn't cool to do so. She wore gauchos long after they were fashionable and has never given up her colorfully patterned, jazzy socks, claiming they make her happy. In hindsight I realize she was not out of touch but merely expressing her creative, adventurous, life-loving attitude. She was doing it her way, and as long as no one got hurt, she didn't see any reason to change the beat she was hearing and happy to march to.

Take the time to explore who you really are this week. Put on those crazy socks, gel your hair, and leave the house. If you're afraid of being labeled weird, this is the exact reason you should go for it. And actually, weird seems to be the new cool. Those who embrace the ways they are different are viewed as strong and confident and know who they are— translation: connected to their beat and marching to their drummer. Take a look at where you have not allowed yourself to be who you truly are, and crack the window open this week.

Step into different; it feels really good! See you next week.

Fourth Sunday in December: Celebrate You

You have been celebrating the season, readying yourself to close another year, and successfully making the connections to move your goals and dreams forward. You have conquered challenges and implemented new life strategies. You understand how to forge ahead to your destiny and can celebrate and recognize the triumph of being on the right path, the individual path you have worked so hard to connect with every day.

You now realize that your own skin is the best fit and requires no alterations. You are receptive to the fact that there is only one you. You cannot be duplicated, and you are a duplicate of no one and nothing else. You have arrived at basking in the light and understanding the connection to yourself and others. The work is not finished, but you cradle the willingness to allow continuous transformation and connection. Bathing in this light is to realize your great power. Take this week to delight and bask in the glow of successfully exploring and connecting to the many varied frontiers during this past year.

Celebrate them all; celebrate you.

The Culmination, A.K.A. the Continuum

....

The culmination of this year completes one full cycle and one piece that will fit snugly into the puzzle of you. This is one-tenth of a decade and one-hundredth of a century, so there is still time, yet time is limited. And so it goes. You have finished, yet you have barely started, and there is the continuum. The journey has been conquered, but there is still more road to travel; goals have been met and now the goalposts have moved.

You have prepared and now opened your repository, readying you to live a more connected life. Enjoy the ability to connect, and best of all, to live harmoniously with your connection, for now you are less encumbered and acutely more aware. By focusing on your gratitude, you have connected to more abundance; through playing you have connected to your inner child, and you have independently navigated what is best for you. You have moved from the vortex of self-criticism and denial into the vortex of living your life gently, benevolently, and compassionately. The rhetoric in your mind has been quelled, giving into the sweet lullabies of confidence that coincide with the determination and ability to conquer anything on your path through connecting to your terms, your boundaries.

Celebrate the joy to disconnect and reconnect while nurturing many connections as your life continues to blossom! Celebrate the knowledge that when you understand your truth, no permission or apology is needed. Welcome to the panoramic view at the top of the mountain and the unobstructed view of your connections to:

your grace,
your glory,
your journey,
your jubilation,
your present, and
your future.

Travel well, xo!